STRANGE HOURS

STRANGE HOURS
Photography, Memory, and the Lives of Artists

SELECTED WRITINGS BY REBECCA BENGAL

An Aperture Ideas Book

aperture

Contents

Foreword
Joy Williams
8

The World of Judith Joy Ross
12

Slowly, and with Much Expression
22

William Gedney's Restless Youth
38

A Brightness I Had Never Seen:
Diana Markosian in Santa Barbara
46

Her Own Private Iowa
54

I Want My People to Remember
Themselves: Richard Throssel and
Horace Poolaw
58

Rewriting "The Ballad":
A Conversation with Nan Goldin
68

Photography's Fiction of Truth:
Yevgenia Belorusets and the Power
of Ambiguity
82

In the Place Where Prince Lived 90

Trail Blaze in an Electrifying Blur: 106
Ming Smith and Her Muses

Close Up the Honky Tonks: Henry 112
Horenstein in 1970s Nashville

The Enormity of the Moment: 120
Life and Death on
an Argentinian Farm

And the Clock Waits So Patiently 132

Chauncey Hare's Protest 150

Picturing the Past-Present: 160
A Visit with Dawoud Bey in Brooklyn

Strange Hours: William Eggleston 170
in Memphis, William Eggleston
in New York City

The Jeremys: A Short Story 184
for Justine Kurland's "Girl Pictures"

Index 195

Acknowledgments 211

Credits 215

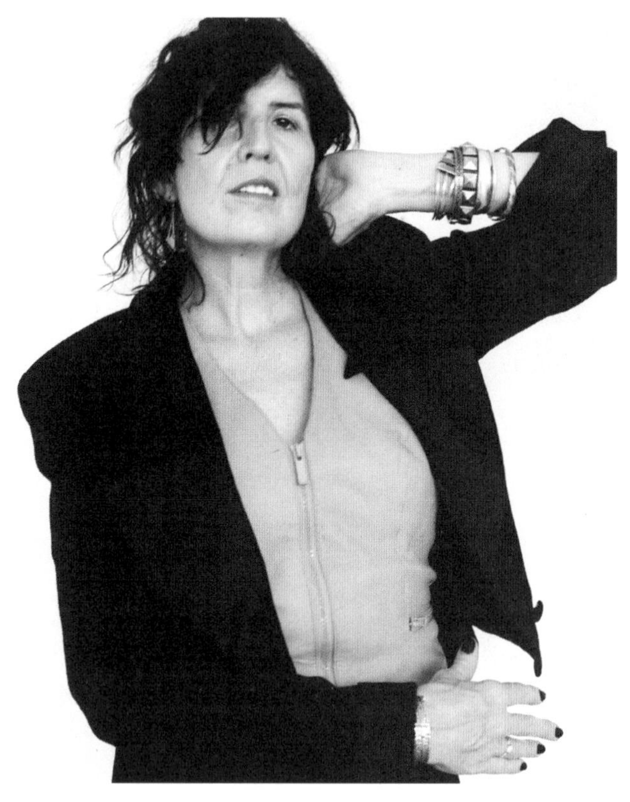

Rebecca Bengal, Brooklyn, October 2022. Photograph by Matthew Leifheit

Foreword
Joy Williams

The great Glenn Gould didn't want to be Glenn Gould. He wanted to be the piano, the Steinway, the instrument that spoke to Bach, spoke to the gods of music. He hated the idea of being between Bach and the Steinway. If he could be the piano Glenn Gould would be absolutely unnecessary.

I've always found this desire exhilarating but impossible to apply to other artistic disciplines. Of course Gould was an interpreter, a performer, creator of the already created. Still, a writer would not wish to be the pencil (and certainly not the computer). Nor would the painter want to be the goopy brush. The sculptor is not the stone realized. The dancer is already the dance. Photographers, one might think, could be an exception and prone to harbor such mystical desire, eliminating the self, becoming one with the other—they are nothing after all without the implement they employ, the camera—but they seem not so inclined. They seem more intent than other artists to espouse process, excess (the making and perusal of hundreds, of thousands of prints), editing and trimming, while simultaneously relying on instinct, spontaneity, and chance.

To write about a writer who writes about photographers is to be at a considerable remove. No being the piano here! The photographs that accompany Rebecca Bengal's texts in *Strange Hours* make an often elusive, if satisfying, pairing with her nimble insights, interviews, encounters, and assessments of an eclectic range of artists from brash William Eggleston to melancholy William Gedney, from the rough downtown hipster scene of Nan Goldin to the Argentine animals in the work of Alessandra Sanguinetti.

More than forty years ago Museum of Modern Art curator John Szarkowski divided photographers into two camps—"mirrors" and "windows." The mirrors were romantic and expressionistic, the windows realistic. Realism of course is a wobbly concept and Szarkowski's cutting of the pie might be disputed, but there is a prominent divide between a decorative and ironic style and the sociological activist and individualistic one. One of the artists represented at the time, Chauncey Hare, protested the exhibit. A perceived window who wanted his work to elicit a "spiritual awakening," he was mostly upset that the show was underwritten by a tobacco company. Another window showcased in *Strange Hours* is the street portraitist Dawoud Bey, who desires to "reinscribe the past" in the presence of his subjects' present, to visualize "*who it was they never got to become*." Judith Joy Ross, a window par excellence, confesses to "rapt, intense, wholehearted belief in the individual." Considered a master of the formal portrait, Ross now prefers to photograph trees.

An illuminating essay on the Native American photographers Richard Throssel and Horace Poolaw, born a generation apart, shows the validity of conflicting approaches—a lyrical engagement with an imposed historical narrative and the freedom of play and pride in mocking those same narratives.

William Eggleston is neither window nor mirror, or you could say he busts up both. He brought color to serious photography after all—vulgar banal color and a regard for vulgar banal subjects as well. Bengal points out that his places and objects are "frequently more autobiographically revelatory than his people." Eggleston himself thinks of his work as "architectural," "abstract."

Two of the longer pieces here address an even bigger divide among photographers, those who think words enhance photographs and enjoy putting together photobooks and songbooks with captions, addendums, and text, and those who certainly do not. *Let Us Now Praise Famous Men* is the flawed iconic storybook, "the one on which so many others are based," but the marriage of Walker Evans and James Agee, Image and Word, was certainly not made in heaven. Putting aside the peculiarity that only three white tenant farming families appeared in the book to the near total exclusion of the predominantly Black residents of Hale County, Alabama, Evans and Agee had jarringly different styles and manners of engagement. "Agee strayed wild and eccentric and rhapsodic in his portrayal," Bengal writes, "while Evans essentially played the straight man, making photographs in the classic, declarative mode that is his legacy. Agee lived with the families, immersing himself in their lives to the point of fantasizing about them ... Set to Agee's besotted words, Evans's photographs disarm with their formal brilliance and ground the narrative in the appearance of realism."

It turned out that neither approach would please the people depicted.

I'm of the tribe that pictures don't need words to substantiate them, though the people who make them frequently do. The tribe that even in these sophisticated tech-slick times believes there's something spooky about camera capture, that a camera can see the very absence of what it views, that it possesses the promise, through voodoo moves, of glimpsing the ghost that is time eternal. Sometimes a photograph can hold legions of freighted and horrid and wordless meaning. Sometimes, say of a photograph of a ceiling painted a lurid red with attendant dangling light bulb, is just a photograph of a red-painted ceiling with a dangling light bulb. And sometimes, ideally, it can be both at once.

Tucson, November 2022

Joy Williams is the author of several collections of short stories and essays, and four novels, including *The Quick and the Dead* (2010) and *Harrow* (2021).

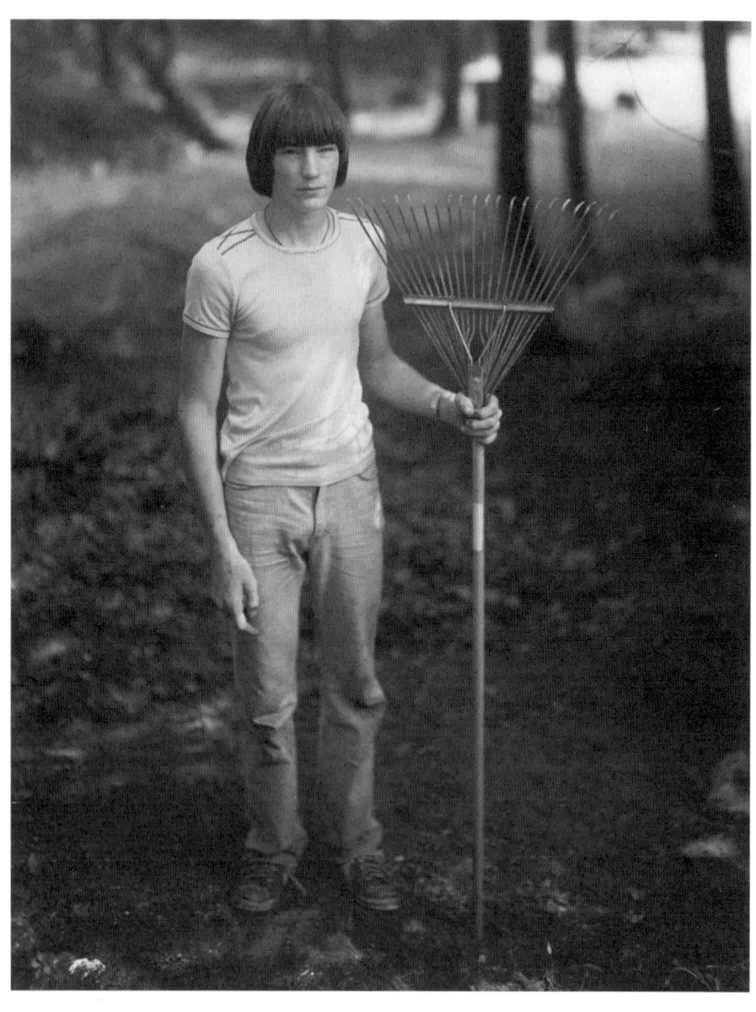

Judith Joy Ross, *Untitled*, Eurana Park, Weatherly, Pennsylvania, 1982

The World of Judith Joy Ross

Judith Joy Ross wants to show me her garden. As she throws open the back door to her home in Bethlehem, Pennsylvania, a large brown rabbit flashes across the yard, a comet trail vanishing into a maze of plants vivid and green against the gray sky. Ross turns to me, her face bright with excitement, "Did you see that?" I am reminded of a story I had heard, how once, while driving in rural Pennsylvania, Ross had seen something in a kid's face that caused her to pull the car over abruptly, drag her 8-by-10 camera out of the car, and call after two boys, aged twelve or so. Within moments, as Ross disappeared under the cloth and the boys began to arrange themselves before her lens, the alchemy of their connection became palpable.

Those particular photographs did not materialize—there was a problem with the film that day—but the Judith Joy Ross pictures that do survive are the representation of thousands of such lightning encounters dating back to the late 1970s and first widely introduced at the 1985 *New Photography* exhibition at the Museum of Modern Art in New York. Ross is a master of the formal portrait, executed with astonishing emotional clarity, as if she could see straight into the innermost lives of the earnest schoolchildren and tormented teenagers, the ennobled gas station attendants and car rental reps, along with veterans, senators, mourners, and protesters, most of them in the

United States, most of them not far from Hazleton, Pennsylvania, the former coal-mining town where she was born and raised. These people form her photographic universe. "She has this extraordinary antenna," former MoMA curator Susan Kismaric, who has worked closely with Ross over the years, told me recently. Kismaric was along for the ride when Ross was photographing in Minersville. "Judith never projects, she never condescends or judges, but she intuits."

In person, Ross is gentle, emphatically honest, devastatingly funny, frequently cursing—all at once. White blunt-cut bangs frame her face; she wears glasses in an outdated prescription. She rarely is idle for long, but when a thought overtakes her, she is apt to rest her entire head in her hands to fully consider it. She greets me on the porch of her yellow house, which, much to her dismay, overlooks construction that will soon obscure her view of Bethlehem, where she has lived for more than half her life. Inside is a home wholly devoted to photography, from the darkroom in the basement to the archives in the attic. "I long for two thousand square feet to store all this shit," she says. There is a large computer monitor in the dining room; its table holds recent contact prints. For her major retrospective, set to open in September at Fundación Mapfre in Madrid, and travel through Europe,* custom photographic paper was made to replace the now discontinued printing-out paper Ross relied on for years.

In the early 1980s, when photographers could simply show up in person on an appointed day at MoMA and drop off their portfolios for review, Ross was called in to speak with John Szarkowski, the photography department's director, who, looking at her first major series, *Eurana Park* (1982), asked if she knew the pictures of the German photographer August Sander. Ross lied and said she didn't. "I was like Judas denying Christ," she says. "I didn't want him to think I was cheating." Szarkowski, who bought two of the pictures, offered reassurance: "It's okay, Judith. It's called tradition to be influenced by another's work." She had, in fact, studied Sander's pictures closely—how he photographed straightforwardly,

                                    THE WORLD OF JUDITH JOY ROSS

centering the person in the frame. Sander's monumental series *Menschen des 20 Jahrhunderts* (People of the 20th Century), begun in the 1920s and proceeding for decades, identified and grouped subjects by occupation and social class. Ross isn't nearly as taxonomic; she is guided by a rapt, intense, wholehearted belief in the individual. (Ross disputes that Sander categorized people.) Her idiosyncratic printing practice—contact prints on printing-out paper that are then toned with gold—enhances the fundamental uniqueness of the individuals she encounters. "No two prints by Judith are the same," says Joshua Chuang, who is curating Ross's retrospective and editing the accompanying catalog. "Her way of experiencing humanity is through photography."

When she was coming up, Ross entered a world dominated by the iconographic portraits of Richard Avedon, Irving Penn, and Diane Arbus, pictures often first published in magazines, where they had to leap off the page. Ross's work, in a range of subtler tones, operates differently. Her contact prints are almost never bigger than the 8-by-10 dimensions of the negative. To enlarge them, she believes, could be "exploitive." Of the prints' scale and intimacy, Ross says, "They are asking you to come closer, and say hi."

"Like Diane Arbus and like Lisette Model, Arbus's teacher, she is working with the idea of the self, the tension between who one is and who one projects to the world," Kismaric explains. "With Arbus, one still sees something of that struggle; in Judith's pictures, outside the cosmopolitan world, it feels as though they're working against futures that were prescribed for them. The questions become more complicated."

Just as complicated is the question of why a photographer so revered by other photographers remains, to an extent, under the radar. The photographer An-My Lê once recalled how, when Ross visited her in New York, she'd play a game of guessing who on the subway Ross would choose to photograph; the fact that she was always wrong cemented Lê's awareness of Ross's empathic intuition. "Her work is beautiful in its transparency," Robert Adams writes in his book *Why People Photograph*—it's "a record of compassion." Gregory Halpern, a photographer who teaches at the Rochester Institute of Technology, has called her "the greatest portrait photographer to have ever worked in the medium." The photographer Paul Graham, who has taught with Ross at Yale, fell first for her Vietnam Veterans Memorial pictures. "It's one of the dirty little secrets of photography," he told me recently. "People act like they want to photograph rocks and houses and trees but what they really want is to have the gumption to photograph people the way Judith does."

Photobooks dominate Ross's shelves along with images by friends, such as Chris Killip, who died in October 2020. "I can't understand how his pictures can be so beautiful," she exclaims. "Tiny little people shown this big, yet every one of them is seen as an individual! Such humanity. Oh, my God. He is missed." Cabinets in nearly every room are filled with boxes of prints and negatives. To a visitor, the house can feel like the brain's memory chambers. Ross claims her own memory is foggy, but whenever a gap emerges, she herds me upstairs to look through the cabinets of boxes of prints to supply the story.

Above her dresser, framed works by her heroes mingle with family pictures. "That's our summer home, where my heart is," she says, pointing at a photograph of a cabin in the borough of Weatherly, Pennsylvania, where Ross grew up daydreaming and playing with her brothers among the creatures in the woods. "That's my mom, that's my dad, that's my Atget," she says, pointing out a print of the Panthéon, a revered gift from her brother Edward. The influence of the French photographer is evident in a few of Ross's early personal pictures: One of her mother, a piano teacher, shown in profile, "looking with some sadness at jewelry at the Met," on a trip she and Ross had taken to New York. One of her father, reclining on a forest floor, dressed in a suit, appears romantic and elegiac. "Fucking suit and a tie in the woods!" Ross says, laughing. It could have been made after a day at the five-and-dime store he owned in Nanticoke, a former mining town where other relatives also had shops selling candy and secondhand books. "He used

     THE WORLD OF JUDITH JOY ROSS

to let me help out, paint faces on the mannequins," she recalls. "I'd put eyeliner on them; I made them even worse. But he never minded. He just wanted us nearby."

Ross made her first photographs in the mid-1960s as a student at Moore College of Art and Design, in Philadelphia. At the IIT Institute of Design in Chicago, where she earned an MA in photography in 1970, she felt disconnected from Aaron Siskind's experimental-minded program. "I was lost," she says. "Eventually, I didn't go to class. Including the Literature of Alienation. I should have gotten at least a C because I never went. I mean, what's wrong with these people!" The lost feeling lingered for a decade. Ross went to Bethlehem, where she taught at what was then known as Moravian College, simultaneously giving herself the photography education she felt she never received in school, via Eastman Kodak materials and the exhibitions she'd see (Arbus and Bruce Davidson, among others) and books she'd buy (Sander, Atget, Lewis Hine) in New York, two hours away. Eventually, she began photographing again.

In 1982, the devastation she felt over her father's death carried her back in time. The beloved summer cabin was lonesome in his absence. Ross took her recently purchased 8-by-10 view camera a few miles away, to a public swimming park in Weatherly. In her mind, the children and teenagers she met there at Eurana Park represented a time of innocence before the first experience of grief. The pictures are holy in their awkwardness—the teen with the dark gothic bangs wielding a rake, the way the girls clasp their hands over their bathing suits—barely visible surroundings briefly lifting them out of their lives. In some, droplets of water can still be seen on skin, evidence of how quickly Ross must have forged these connections.

"I photographed people from the get-go. Even though I didn't know how to have them in my life. That's probably why I'm good at it," Ross says. "Something happens, I see them intensely, and we never see each other again. I know it's just a photograph. I know I'm being delusional. But I like to think I'm capturing the real thing."

"But if you didn't think that it was the real thing in the moment, could you even make the picture?" I ask. Ross shakes her head emphatically, no.

Over the years, the arc of her work has expanded in scope to wider communities, public institutions, and national politics, projects for which Ross has sometimes earnestly sought the permission of mayors and civic organizations. But the true subject is both as simple and complicated as every human she meets. In 1983, thinking she would do a series about the United States and the Vietnam War, she traveled to Maya Lin's granite memorial in Washington, DC, and found herself drawn to solitary expressions of grief.

The distinctions between her projects became apparent in her printing techniques. "In Eurana Park, certain browns were happy," Ross says. "When kids were pubescent they turned gray. For me, I didn't get puberty. I wasn't a happy camper with sexuality." Tones for Ross exist on a psychological register, darkening or morphing over time. "Certainly Vietnam was gray. And the gray got so extreme. Pictures from Nanticoke, they might be an exquisite gray with a dash of purple in it that was melancholy. Or a brown shadow on a gray print. A gray print means something."

In 1986, armed with a Guggenheim grant, one good suit, a makeshift shopping cart for her equipment, including a suspicious-looking box swathed in duct tape to hold her camera, and an inborn fear of authority figures, Ross set out for Capitol Hill—"gray with highlights and a hint of brown in the shadow." She photographed Strom Thurmond "with his five-foot-tall shoulders and shrunken apple head, surrounded by his French furniture… This awful racist person, but I was seduced by his presence." Her skill at creating instantaneous connections, and the magic ritual of bringing out the view camera, were crucial in these fifteen-minute appointments. In the faces of the members of Congress, humanized in Ross's frame, it is possible to glimpse, briefly, an aspect of their private selves, not far removed from her young swimmers and workers back in Pennsylvania.

     THE WORLD OF JUDITH JOY ROSS

In the early 1990s, when money was tight, Ross began cleaning houses. "Does it look like I'd be a good maid?" she joked, waving at her stacks of archival boxes. "I carried superglue with me on the job; I broke everything." It was in the midst of this time that the photographer John Gossage called to tell her she'd won a Charles Pratt Memorial Award of $25,000. First, she retorted, "How do I know you're John Gossage?" and then she called the owners of the house she was supposed to clean that day to say she wasn't coming. "I'm Cinderella! I just got a grant!"

From 1992 through 1994, she returned to the same public schools in Hazleton she'd daydreamed through while growing up. Again, the goal was idealistic. "I wanted people to pay their taxes. I wanted people to care about public education," Ross says. "I certainly didn't care about mine. I thought school sucked." Ross's Hazleton pictures are singular in their acknowledgment that school can indeed suck, and in their eerily personal portrayal of the vastness and discomfort and yearning and angst of adolescence—the pride of a perfectly brushed mullet or a cascade of sprayed hair. "These are *their own selves*," she says. In a print displayed in her front room, a boy stares at the camera through glasses so thick you long to tell him they'll be considered cool in twenty years. But here, he is simply a high schooler briefly showing his vulnerable self. Ross's framing preserves this, acting as a protective shell.

Protest the War (2007), an unassuming little book published by Steidl and Pace/MacGill, her gallery at the time, is about the size of a trucker's logbook or a horse-racing pamphlet. Ross, hoping the pictures could change people's minds about who a nonviolent protester is, had wished it would be distributed at gas stations, "right next to the chewing tobacco and the beef jerky and the breath mints." The fervent, believing expressions of her protesters never made it into this montage, but Ross herself again went to Capitol Hill, hand delivering copies at congressional offices. At the heart of her work is a profound identification with the singular person and a belief in what society can and should be, the rift that exists between the two, and the person confronting the specter of change. "I see you, and, please God, I want to get what I see before it's gone," Ross says. "Once you get out the camera, you get discombobulated and you have to find it again. You may not be finding the same thing."

Ross says she is not interested in photographing people anymore. Or, that she does have a new idea about photographing people that she is intent on pursuing, but she doesn't want to talk about it yet in a public way. She is recovering from eye surgery that she claims made her vision worse. The world has been so uncertain.

Last year, in the days before the US presidential election was called, Ross began to photograph trees. "Maybe it's sacrilegious to talk about them this way, but I do see them not as people but as individuals," she says. We get in Ross's car, stickered MAKE AMERICA GREEN AGAIN, and she points out favorite elms as we drive to a cemetery in Bethlehem, from which you can glimpse, through a veil of ropy vines, the cemetery that Walker Evans famously depicted in *A Graveyard and Steel Mill in Bethlehem, Pennsylvania* (1935). "He couldn't have photographed from here, because everything's the same tone," she notes. Ross comes here for walks, not pictures. "The subject of death is so enormous, who can photograph it?"

She is pleased when I notice that, instead of camera equipment packed in her car, an animal cage rests on the backseat. Later, I will think how *cage* or *trap* feels like the wrong word, especially for someone who lights up when she describes seeing a muskrat in the wild and tells me she cannot bear to have dogs anymore ("because you love them more than your family, of course"), especially when I learn that it is for the groundhog that lives under her porch and sometimes ventures to the back steps, standing on its hind legs. She speaks of it in a way, I think, that might apply to some of the people in her pictures: "Sometimes, I think I should try to catch it," Ross says, "and take it to a happier place."

In September 2001, Ross began to make portraits at another site of mourning—an overlook on the Eagle Rock Reservation

                                        THE WORLD OF JUDITH JOY ROSS

in New Jersey where people come to stare toward New York at the spot where the Twin Towers once stood. Silently, Ross would slip a handwritten request to anyone she wished to photograph. A day after our visit, I drive to Eagle Rock. I try to pick out the people whom Ross might approach, and I am sure I am wrong. On my way out, I notice a young couple walking rapidly away from a marshy thicket, carrying a long trap seemingly identical to the one I'd seen in Ross's car. The cage is empty; whatever they have brought with them, they have now released.

*Editor's note: The exhibition *Judith Joy Ross* was presented by Fundación Mapfre in Madrid, September 24, 2021–January 9, 2022.

Originally published in *Aperture*, issue 244, "Cosmologies," Fall 2021.

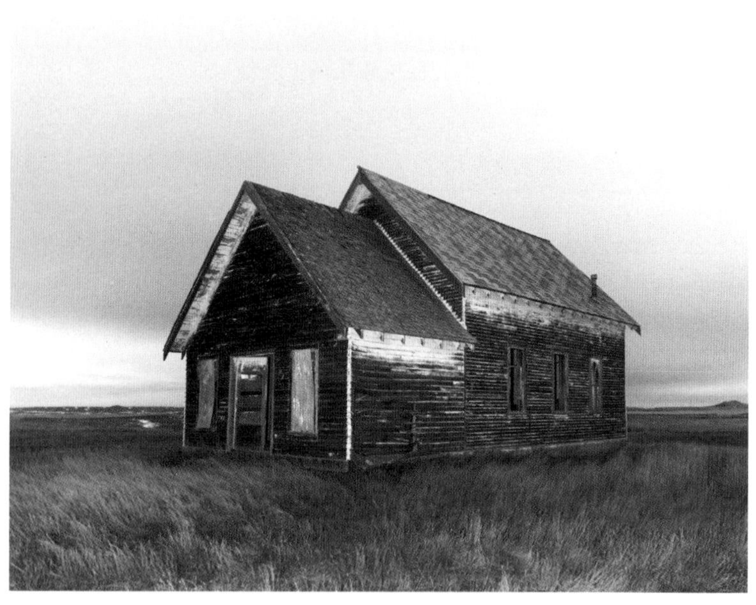

Alec Soth, *Near Williston, North Dakota*, 2012

Slowly, and with Much Expression

I

My father was born profoundly Deaf, like his brother and father and many generations before them. He does not read lips, he communicates in American Sign Language and written English and also, among certain relatives, in a unique family sign language created in the 1800s by our Deaf and hearing ancestors, who needed a way of communicating on an isolated farm in western North Carolina. Never in his entire life has my father heard any sound whatsoever, nor does he particularly want to—Deafness is part of who he is and how he experiences the world, he points out, and he has no desire to attempt to change that, through cochlear implants or magic wands or otherwise.

Among the things that have transformed his experience of the world, however, is the invention of closed captioning, the arrival of which in our household was as momentous for him as, say, MTV was for my sister and me. His TV tastes run to sports, the news, a lot of action movies, a lot of comedy, especially physical and slapstick, dramatically expressive stuff that you can get the general drift of without sound. For a while our family had two televisions, side by side, one muted and captioned, the other with the volume up (my mother, my sister, and I are all hearing) and a wordless screen; and our split focus shifted back and forth between two screens, two modes. Captioning explained things my dad had previously guessed at—here, now, revealed, were whole passages of dialogue surrounding a gag in a rerun of *I Love Lucy* he remembered from childhood; here, spilling across the screen in black-barred type, was some typist's interpretation of a sitcom sound effect—ZRRBRRTTT, the caption would bleat—or what might have otherwise been alluded to—[KISSING SOUNDS]. Subtle moments missed in other films were suddenly illuminated and made comprehensible; plots were clarified; gaps were filled; mysteries were solved; the visual world was explained. Was it made larger, I have later wondered, or smaller? Was the reveal so drastic and great, each telling now existed as two separate stories, with two separate meanings?

II

There are multiple ways to approach Alec Soth's *Songbook* (2015), which sits in your hands like a slightly oversized hymnal or collection of sheet music, its dimensions ostensibly deliberately askew from either of those things. The pea-green cloth binding, the practically floral typeface of title and photographer's name, the bit of notation and lyrics printed on the back, from Howard Dietz and Arthur Schwartz's "Dancing in the Dark" ("We're waltzing in the wonder of why we're here / Time hurries by / We're here") with the direction *slowly, and with much expression*—all point at the Great American Songbook, the canon of twentieth-century pop standards, by turns hopeful or morose, swooning, hokey, expansive. "Georgia On My Mind." "Moon River." "All of Me." "Santa Claus Is Coming to Town."

Swollen, marshmallow-white clouds puff out over the rooftop of an abandoned motel as if on the verge of engulfing it, and if that sounds a little pearly-gates heavenly, a few plates later, another motel: the word *JESUS* has been skywritten overhead, perhaps just escaping the attention of a patron clad only in a pair of long printed shorts, flip-flopping back into his room maybe to fetch a beverage to enjoy in the standard-issue white plastic chair he's dragged out into a parking space. (Will *JESUS* still be legible when he returns? Will it have partially evaporated, vanished, simply, to *US*?) There are recurrent flip-flops, recurrent motels, recurrent churches. In what appears to be a church basement, in a strange yet chaste scene, a teenage girl dressed in denim cutoffs and flip-flops boogies some several feet away from a priest wearing shirtsleeves and a backwards collar. In another photograph, in some other room somewhere, a man dances all alone, a large smile on his face. There are recurrent, somber processions: a family in orthodox dress walking along a roadside at night. Texas rangers filing in line for an execution. There are recurrent lonesome rooms so lonesome that no one is in them; there are recurrent lonesome structures looking very much in danger of being swallowed up by the natural world: swarms of kudzu preying on a farmhouse. That cloud-surrounded motel. Verse, chorus, verse. Elsewhere, recurrent lonesome figures inhabit vast-seeming scenes, fields and woods and bedrooms. The fields become larger, the figures smaller. *Slowly, and with much expression.*

Those very familiar with Soth's work will no doubt recognize many of these from another project, but more on that in a minute; for now, consider *Songbook* as songbook, photobook as songbook: Soth placing himself in the role of yesteryear composer. His photographs may not exactly be the songs sung by lovesick girls waiting on porch swings for their soldier beaux, or by improbably tap-dancing fellows making their way down rainy streets, but they are of that world, and certainly they are of those individuals who exist just on its borders. Musicality exists also in the visible yearning for connection and communion that is palpable in the most solitary of these photographs, even if it's simply a hand tossing an object to another hand or that kudzu, creeping ever closer to the front porch.

Soth's best-known photobooks to date, *Sleeping by the Mississippi*, *Niagara*, *Broken Manual*, *The Last Days of W.*, and the books he publishes under his imprint Little Brown Mushroom, share an abiding interest in the way words and images work together—or choose to work alone. "I've never necessarily loved the two together," he told me recently on the phone. *Songbook* isn't overly wordy, but throughout are smatterings of verses from the Great American Songbook lyricists—Cole Porter, Johnny Mercer, Sammy Cahn. Soth has muted the words that in another life once accompanied these photographs, replaced them with sparse, wistful, and earnest lyrics. Out of context, their meaning becomes larger and ambiguous: you can imagine any number of stories happening here.

"Well, I cheated a little," Soth told me. "I needed to nudge the interpretation away from the literal side of the story. Muting the words felt great in many ways. I was freed to bathe in the music of it. Like, I can just cruise on it. I can just be a photographer. It was liberating."

III

In terms of his own photography, Walker Evans, a French lit major whose great influences were Flaubert and Baudelaire (before he fell for the photographs of Eugène Atget, whose work he once said "sang like lightning") was "interested in what any present time will look like as the past," as he wrote in the introduction to the 1962 reissue of *American Photographs*. Evans was also one half of photography and writing's great and flawed twentieth-century storybook, the one on which so many others are based: *Let Us Now Praise Famous Men*, with James Agee. The book was as radical for what it did not do—it went against everything one is taught since reading "picture books" as a child, rejecting the assumption that images exist to directly represent words—as for what it did do, which was to tell a story in which images and words were equals, but did not necessarily have a literal connection. Charged with that dual responsibility, each was free to wander, while also bound

   SLOWLY, AND WITH MUCH EXPRESSION

to respond to the other, ostensibly aiming for a narrative balance.

Like a vaudeville duo—in which Agee strayed wild and eccentric and rhapsodic in his portrayal of a few tenant farming families in Depression-era Alabama—Evans essentially played the straight man, making photographs in the classic, declarative mode that is his legacy. Agee lived with the families, immersing himself in their lives to the point of fantasizing about them; Evans apparently took a room in town. Set to Agee's besotted words, Evans's photographs disarm with their formal brilliance and ground the narrative in the appearance of realism. To see the photographs as "definitive" and Agee's prose as relatively subjective, however, endows them with a dangerous power—to assume their close-up work with three white tenant families is "true" of the place ignores a wide swath of humanity in Hale County, Alabama, whose population at the time was overwhelmingly majority Black. As Agee writes in the book, "I notice how much slower white people are to catch on than negroes, who understand the meaning of a camera, a weapon, a stealer of images and souls, a gun, an evil eye." Many of the families and the descendants of those in the book—whose names Agee changed, but later became known—resisted the way they'd been depicted.

As remarkable as their work is in its multiple forms (including the later discovered smaller book *Cotton Tenants*, published in 2013), the products of their collaboration tell us less today about what that part of the world was like then than how it was seen from outside and how it was shown. The book that came out of what was an assignment for *Fortune* (yet never published by the magazine) is not history but an uncanny merger of fact and fiction, narrative and projection. *Let Us Now Praise Famous Men* defies convention and length and genre and tone, risking and failing and succeeding and surpassing all at once. It is the utterly weird model to which later collaborations of writers and photographers continue to answer and to question; not just documentarians, but all kinds of storytellers. Do pictures need words and if so, what is their responsibility to the other? "Can one think in terms of a truly photographic narrative form?" John Berger writes in *Another Way of Telling*.

Evans's other collaborations are part of the focus of David Campany's *Walker Evans: The Magazine Work*. With Agee, for instance, Evans clandestinely photographed their fellow passengers on a cruise to Havana for the story "Six Days at Sea," which was published by *Fortune*; to accompany a story about William Faulkner running in *Vogue*, he was commissioned to photograph the Southern landscape of the novelist's fictional world. In a kind of call-and-response move, Faulkner, in turn, would be motivated to write a short story based on a photograph of a graveyard by Evans that he had seen; "Sepulture South: Gaslight" would later appear in *Harper's Bazaar*.

Eventually Evans would photograph, write, design, and typeset many of his own magazine stories. "Photography seems to be the most literary of the graphic arts," he once said. It was a sentiment shared by other photographers after him, like William Gedney, whose photographs of the Cornett family in rural Kentucky have much in common with Evans's and Agee's sharecroppers. "I am attempting a literary form in visual terms," Gedney wrote in his notebooks.

IV

The world of the now-defunct *DoubleTake* magazine, started by the doctor, psychiatrist, and author Robert Coles and photographer Alex Harris, was informed by the partnership of Agee and Evans and the heyday of *Fortune*, by the writers and photographers of the Works Progress Administration, and realists and authors of Southern fiction, Flannery O'Connor and Eudora Welty and Walker Percy and Joseph Mitchell, Studs Terkel and Raymond Carver, and numerous Williams (Maxwell, Eggleston, Gedney, William Carlos). Every issue ran the same poem by Seamus Heaney, which includes the lyric, "Call the miracle self-healing: The utter

   SLOWLY, AND WITH MUCH EXPRESSION

self-revealing double-take of feeling." Published quarterly from 1995 to 1999 in conjunction with the Center for Documentary Studies at Duke University, and then less frequently for another five years afterward, it was conceived as "a home where image and word have equal weight."

Even though it drew on a classic lineage, *DoubleTake* was a revelation, with its emphasis on portraying "ordinary" people —Gedney's Kentucky photographs, photographs of factory workers about to be laid off, South Chicago short stories by Stuart Dybek—with its distinctive design, another way of giving images equal treatment and weight. It won a National Magazine Award for general excellence.

In its lesser moments the magazine could be overly earnest, at its best it risked that earnestness and broke through to reveal something else. If it had existed longer, it could have been exciting to see it challenge and question its own influences, and evolve past their inherent limitations—a doubletake on *DoubleTake*. Those of us who worked on it (I was a very young member of its editorial staff for a time) were aware that we were part of something special, and also something ephemeral. It's hard today to describe the impact of the publication: as my former boss once joked to me on the phone, "You mean a magazine with literary fiction and long-form nonfiction about regular people, and photographic essays and poems and book reviews and . . . ?" Put that way, *DoubleTake* doesn't *sound* terribly groundbreaking, yet no one has been able to precisely reproduce it in scope or in feeling. Several other magazines have shared elements of *DoubleTake*'s particular pairing of word and image—notably, Tibor Kalman and Oliviero Toscani's *COLORS*. Every few years, since its demise in the early 2000s, it seems there's yet another well-intentioned magazine, yet these have been pallid resuscitations. It's a shame that no one has quite gotten it since, even in a world that today insists on storytelling, and on reinventing narrative. The confluence of circumstances that made *DoubleTake* possible will not likely recur, so better then to look at its archives, a brief but compelling meditation and record of the possibilities and problems and relationships that exist between words and pictures.

Among those, though, who credit the lingering influence of *DoubleTake* is Soth, who not long ago Instagrammed a throwback picture of himself reading from an issue in which Bruce Springsteen tells Will Percy (nephew of Walker Percy) how he keeps multiple copies of Robert Frank's *The Americans*: "I've always wished I could write songs the way he takes pictures."

V

Soth has worked alone—this is the work he's best known for—and in collaboration: with images solely, and with photographs and text together. For *Iris Garden* (2013) he merged texts by John Cage with photographs from William Gedney's archive, including some of the composer on a mushroom hunt, superimposing a weird, shifting narrative (the text was printed on inserts that can be moved throughout the book, set to different photographs). The book works on its own terms, evocative and strange, hinting at a less studious way for words and pictures to work together, more along the lines of W. G. Sebald's photo-strewn ruminative novels and hybrid essays, more like poems.

With the writer Brad Zellar, Soth made the book *House of Coates* (2012); to accompany the deadpan narrative that both artists purport is written by a vagrant named Lester, Soth made snapshots as if Lester himself were pressing the button on whatever camera he'd managed to wrangle; blurry, bleak roadside sightings. Several years ago, Soth asked Zellar to accompany him on a road trip. Both had newspaper experience lurking in their backgrounds; here, they'd be reporters, essentially, giving themselves imaginary assignments and deadlines, gathering stories, conducting interviews, making photographs of the people and places they encountered. Soth printed up business cards with the name *The Winter Garden Dispatch*, which would eventually become the *LBM Dispatch*, a broadsheet irregularly published by Little Brown Mushroom.

The first state was Minnesota, home turf for both. They went on to travel to Michigan, Colorado, Texas, Georgia, Ohio, as well as more specific yet nebulously mythic-sounding regions, Upstate (New York) and Three Valleys (Silicon, San Joaquin, and Death). Soth, who primarily works in color, photographed in black and white; Zellar's text swung between historical fact, oblique quotes from Willa Cather or William Gibson, and briefly captured stories and moments from the lives of carpet sellers, self-ordained ministers, train-hoppers, yoga instructors, the last snow-globe repairman.

The project was very much after the dark heart of Sherwood Anderson's *Winesburg, Ohio*, and also in the vein of small-town papers, Agee and Evans, or the WPA travel guides, all among the source material they consulted before visiting a new place—assembling an itinerary rooted in the history, literature, music, and idiosyncratic attraction native to the region. It is a classic approach reminiscent of the "shooting scripts" for small towns, cow towns, coal towns, railyards that Roy Stryker, who launched the documentary photography program of the Farm Security Administration, would send as photographer assignments in the Great Depression, objects meant to illustrate ideas. "You must get this feeling of unemployment . . . try to pick up something of the feeling on the side of youth," he instructed an FSA photographer headed to a mining town in Pennsylvania. Among the dozens of entries itemized in Stryker's script for "American Habit," for instance: "Sky writing, Paper in park after concert, Parade watching, ticker tape, sitting on curb, Roller skating—on sidewalk or street, Spooners–neckers." "Park on Sunday," he wrote. "People sitting and sleeping in newspapers." (Perhaps in reaction to Stryker's prescriptions, in a drifting, difficult year or so after *Fortune* rejected their Hale County collaboration, Agee and Evans each wrote their own contrary lists of things they hated. On Evans's itemized list: "The sex life of America . . . Disgust in the boat train. The taxi horns of Paris . . . Tobacco. Solitude." It could have been a worthy project.)

Stryker's lists are ancestors of the ones Soth would tape to his steering wheel when working solo on projects like *Niagara*, his 2006 photobook of aspiration and drowned romance that loitered the motels and bars on either side of the Falls. Soth set his sights by a smattering of quotes from *Lolita* and, as he details in the notes at the end of *Niagara*, an updated catalog of what the roadside might deliver: "high-school yearbooks, Polaroids, men in pajamas." Like Stryker, who saw his scripts as guides to a place and acknowledged the discrepancy between them and what the photographer might encounter in the actual living world, Soth's steering wheel lists begin as guides but quickly become invitations to detour from the intended route.

For the *Dispatch*, the list was more like extant worlds within worlds, and social networks mostly of the old order but also of the new: remote island communities, roadhouses, the Optimist Club, labor camps, the headquarters of Facebook. It was an exploration of loneliness. "There's stuff I'm drawn to because I'm drawn to it," Soth says to me. "With this project, I made a real effort to photograph more broadly. But my people—I can't help it. I'd walk into a room and it might be filled with people, but I'd immediately see that one guy, and Brad would just look at me and sort of sigh and say, 'Go ahead, do your thing.'"

Zellar's stories amplified the photographs and vice versa, each feeding the curiosity inspired by the other. Stories that made you want to see more, photographs that made you want to know more, mysteries and plots elucidated. In a sense, Soth and Zellar's project belongs to a trajectory beyond the simple collaboration of photographer and writer; in that sense they are practitioners of a tenuous, evolving form that blends facts and insists on fiction. And yet, Soth says, "There was a frustration for me in the backstory, in feeling like I had to carry the weight of all these stories."

Before *Niagara* went to press, Soth included handwritten captions and addenda, which appear in the index of images at the end of the book. "I couldn't help myself," he says; the stories

    SLOWLY, AND WITH MUCH EXPRESSION

are there in the photographs, of pawn shops and love letters and cheap honeymoon motels, but these were anecdotes too good to simply let go. Like liner notes for a record album, they opened up the larger story of the book's making, and they stood, also, as stories on their own.

Pictures are luckier, they are looser than words. Words have to fight harder to arrange themselves, to express that which in a photograph might be the mingling of order and accident, a strange convergence, a kind of grace. Or words are luckier, because they can rearrange over time.

Songbook is complete when you arrive at its final image, an outline of a tiny, barely perceptible human figure alone in the midst of what appears to be a tundra, but turns out to be Death Valley. On its facing page is printed the only nonmusical text of the book, by that playwright of solitude and the absurd, Eugène Ionesco. I won't tell you here what Ionesco says. It's really all in the photographs.

VI

The questions you get from people when they learn your father is Deaf: *Does he lip-read?* No. (The shapes of spoken words are attached to the experience of sound.) *Do you know how to sign?* Yes. (How else would we communicate? I began to sign before I could talk.) As a kid I was frustrated at first when I discovered that not every word in English has an exact analog in American Sign Language. Growing up in a bilingual house, in between the hearing and Deaf worlds, my mind had been overtaken by the verbal. But to attempt to sign exact words will yield a stilted, lackluster caption—a Google Translate version of a sentence. True signing can't be seen in a static frame or boiled down to words joined together—signing is expression. From an early age I registered written words as sound—I heard them as I read, as I wrote. I still do. It's still hard for me to speak aloud and sign simultaneously in a very fluid way, say, if I'm trying to tell a story to a Deaf and hearing person in real time. I'll switch up without warning, I'll catch myself filling in gaps between speech with a sign, and vice versa.

As a writer, I have learned to love these gaps—ideally these are the places in a story, or in a film, or in a book of photographs and text where the reader can enter imaginatively, or where words and images can speak to each other. They are the openings every artist should strive for. And yet, when I'm talking and signing, I'm inventing, I'm stalling, I'm creating, I'm fumbling, as we all are, clumsy with language. English words fail me, too, constantly. When I'm searching for a word, I might land on a picture instead.

VII

Denis Johnson's poem "The Throne of the Third Heaven of the Nations' Millennium General Assembly" takes its title from James Hampton, a secret artist originally hailing from Elloree, South Carolina, and his great work, a nearly three-hundred-square-foot installation fantastically ornate and winged crowns, thrones, altars, lecterns, and sculptures made mostly from salvaged furniture and cheap materials, embellished with transformed and painted bits of wine bottle foil and cigarette foil, Reynolds wrap, and colored paper that survived him in Washington, DC. For fourteen years, Hampton rented a garage near the Shaw neighborhood and began work around midnight, after his shift as a janitor in a federal building, creating his staging site for the Second Coming of Christ he believed was nigh. In Johnson's poem, the speaker concludes that Hampton was "probably insane" though it's hard to discern if he really thought so. "I couldn't take it all in," he writes in a few lines that have their own biblical precedent, the language of awe. "And I was a little frightened." *And they were sore afraid.* Hampton received visions; he appointed himself "Director, Special Projects for the State of Eternity." In the

     SLOWLY, AND WITH MUCH EXPRESSION

few photographs of Hampton that survive, he poses among his creation, wearing a black suit, and in one, he tries on one of his own crowns, as if welcoming parishioners to church or ushering them into the afterlife. Johnson's poem, again:

> Photograph me photograph me photo
> Graph me in my suit of loneliness,
> My tic which I have been
> Saving for this occasion

The sculptor Ed Kelly answered a newspaper ad placed by Hampton's pawnbroker landlord who discovered the work after Hampton's death in 1964 from stomach cancer. Eventually Robert Rauschenberg and Harry Lowe, then assistant director of the Smithsonian American Art Museum, were summoned to Hampton's garage studio. "It was like opening Tut's tomb," Lowe told the *Washington Post. The Throne* has remained on view at the Smithsonian since 1970.

Hampton was born in 1909 to Southern tenant farmers. His father, a gospel singer, left home for the road and Hampton fled the fields at nineteen to live with a brother in Washington, DC, and served in the Pacific during World War II. He abandoned the idea of a single church, too; in DC, he went to churches of all denominations and held a solitary service in his own garage. A few actual words exist among the works, the inscription "Fear Not" above the central throne and, tacked to a bulletin board, a verse from Proverbs: "Where there is no vision, the people perish." There were plans and sketches. But also among them: a hundred handwritten pages in a mixture of letters, ciphers, and musical-like notation that two faculty from San José State University have since attempted to decode. It possessed a logic, but an otherworldly one. Eventually, they wrote, they concluded that this "Hamptonese" was the written equivalent of speaking in tongues.

The "unknown script" is one Hampton invented and in which he wrote notes on drawings he made for the works he'd later make, pictures in his mind's eye, a wordless language for an imagined future. How else could one caption a vision? From Johnson's poem:

> He waits forever in front of diagrams
> On a blackboard in one of his photographs
> Labels that make no sense attached
> To the radiant, alien things he sketched,
> Which aren't objects, but plans.

Originally published in *Guernica* on February 2, 2015.

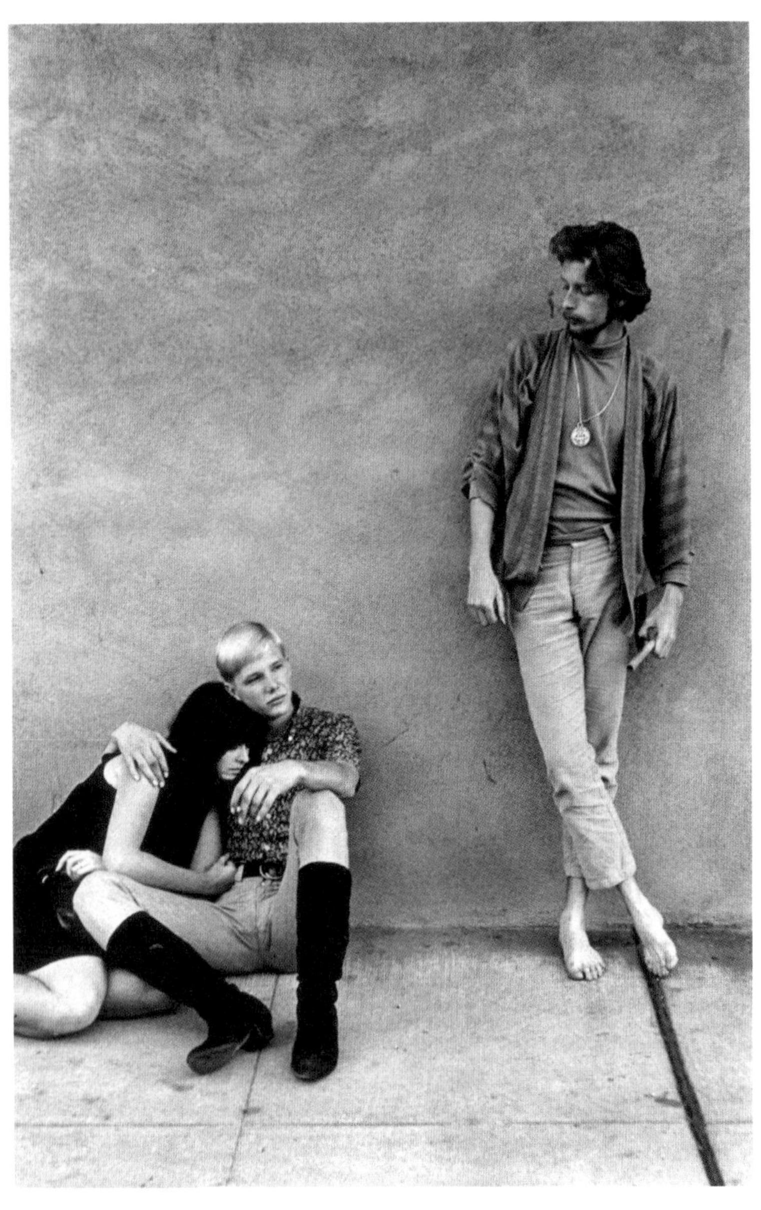

William Gedney, *A Time of Youth: San Francisco*, 1966–1967

William Gedney's Restless Youth

In 1999, when I was an intern at the now-defunct photography and literature quarterly *Double Take*, housed at the Center for Documentary Studies at Duke University, I was asked to proofread a survey of photographs by William Gedney. The revered but little-known artist had died a decade earlier. Since no books of his work had been published in his lifetime, *What Was True: The Photographs of William Gedney*, coedited by Margaret Sartor and Geoff Dyer, would be an introduction for most readers. It certainly was for me. I was struck by the intimacy of Gedney's photographs, the accidentally graceful human arrangements in his black-and-white frames: barefoot, stringy-haired girls loitering in a kitchen near a Kentucky mining camp in the 1960s; a young boy gripping the steering wheel of a stalled car; teenage boys and men gathered, shirtless, around the flipped-up hood of another broken-down car. Gedney's pictures were both secretive and familiar. They spoke to the way I had felt watching grown-ups talk on my grandparents' small mountain farm, when they thought us kids weren't really paying attention. Gedney's pictures let people reveal a hidden part of themselves in a way that other photographs I'd encountered of country people and poor people did not. He saw them with complicated beauty, without condescension. The people in his frames could, and did, desire and dream of worlds and existences beyond what was expected and assumed of them.

In recognizing that quality, the photographer simultaneously revealed something of his own longing.

Gedney worked this way, whether photographing young seekers dropping out of life and making their way to San Francisco in the sixties, or people on the streets of India in the early seventies, or the regulars in a dingy, raucous bar in his Brooklyn neighborhood—which, many years later, would become mine too. His people-less photographs—of cars parked on empty streets and lonesome dark yards at night reflect human feeling. Just as palpable as the melancholy that pervades his pictures is a sense of camaraderie, a physical freedom among people nonetheless simultaneously harboring deep and private worries. The bonds between them showed in a dozen subtle, alluring ways, and Gedney captured them in multitudes, sometimes within a single frame.

William Gale Gedney was born in 1932 and grew up in rural upstate New York. At nineteen he enrolled at Pratt Institute in Brooklyn, where he majored in graphic design but discovered what he would call "a natural feeling for photography." In order to make his photographs on his own terms, Gedney lived frugally. For years, he made do in a cold-water flat in Brooklyn close to Pratt, filled with books and music and his steadily growing, meticulously organized archives. He picked up paying work at Time-Life Books and Condé Nast Publications; later, he taught at Pratt and Cooper Union, working jobs that were either temporary or that he'd quit when he saved enough money.

According to his friends, Gedney had a loud, bellowing laugh. To his friend and onetime-lover, writer Joseph Caldwell, Gedney jokingly claimed to be descended from "reindeer thieves." About his photographs, though, he was absolutely serious. Maria Friedlander has written that Gedney had "often expressed his feeling that to be a truly committed artist one had to be free to pursue one's work." He was a "loner, very private," she wrote. At least in certain circles, he kept his love life closely guarded. Once, when she asked him if he wanted to get married, if he'd ever had a close girlfriend, he answered with that same bellowing

                    WILLIAM GEDNEY'S RESTLESS YOUTH

laugh, one that Friedlander came to understand meant that she had "come upon a gate that he kept firmly closed." In his 2019 memoir, *In the Shadow of the Bridge*, Caldwell recalls meeting Gedney in 1959 as they passed each other on the Brooklyn Bridge (the subject of a series Gedney was working on). They soon began an affair and exchanged apartment keys, but this relationship eventually dissolved as Gedney became consumed again with his art. When they reconnected again as friends in the mid-1980s, Gedney was visibly ill, covered in lesions from Kaposi's sarcoma. He was living in the first and only house he owned, a fixer-upper on Staten Island where, under his care, a grape arbor, a cherry tree, and a vegetable garden flourished. He had also "semi-adopted" a German shepherd mix he named Mr. Dog. Caldwell, who had been volunteering support for patients through the Gay Men's Health Crisis, would move in as caretaker. He was at Gedney's side when he died at fifty-six years old, in 1989.

In another world, one in which Gedney was allowed to live longer, or was exhibited more frequently, his name likely would be widely mentioned today alongside those who championed his work. This would include Walker Evans, who recommended Gedney for his Guggenheim grant in 1966; his friend Diane Arbus, who encouraged him to take over the teaching of her classes at Cooper Union; John Szarkowski, who gave him a solo exhibition at the Museum of Modern Art in 1968, which the curator described as a study of "people living precariously under difficulty." Maria and Lee Friedlander remained close to Gedney throughout his life and were among those who helped arrange for the acquisition of Gedney's archives by the special collections library at Duke University, including thousands of finished prints and seven handmade maquettes of the books Gedney never published in his lifetime.

"They seem to be doing happy things sadly, or maybe they're doing sad things happily." This enigmatic observation by John Cage, another friend of the photographer, is one of only two brief texts that William Gedney included in an unpublished maquette that he titled *A Time of Youth*. Photographed in San Francisco over the course of ninety-nine days, from October 1966 to early 1967, the series is a witness to a time before a time—the preamble to the Summer of Love, transitory and searching, and refreshingly devoid of any grooviness or flower-power tropes that would later be implanted in collective memory. *A Time of Youth: San Francisco, 1966–1967* (2021), published fifty-some years since its inception, marks the first book devoted to a single, complete project by the photographer. About half the book is devoted to supplementary texts—pages from Gedney's letters and journals, and in-depth essays by critic Philip Gefter and the book's editor, Lisa McCarty. But at the core is Gedney's maquette of eighty-nine images, revealing him as a prescient creator of the modern, lyrical photobook, which he saw as a unique literary genre. "I worked for the collective impression," Gedney wrote in April 1969, "yet tried to make each of the individual pictures stand on their own." He envisioned the photographs as elements in a story and sequenced them so that they progressed from morning to night—effectively collapsing his eighty-nine days into a semi-fictional twenty-four hours. In this way, he was as ahead of his time artistically as the young dropouts and hippies who had arrived on the cusp of the counterculture. *A Time of Youth* offers the first opportunity to see his long-form work close to the way he conceived of it—as a dramatic narrative formed almost entirely by the pictures.

McCarty writes that, although she added essays and con-textual materials, she otherwise tried to hew to the specifica-tions in Gedney's notes, including the book's sequence. She enlarged the dimensions slightly (the book measures nine by nine inches; Gedney desired eight by eight). Compared to his luminous Kentucky photographs, the San Francisco work tends to be darker in emotional tenor and denser in tonality, with semi-obscured figures and downturned, daydreaming faces. *A Time of Youth* feels kindred to "Slouching Towards Bethlehem," Joan Didion's landmark essay depicting the grimmer, disillusioned side of Haight-Ashbury, as if Gedney and Didion had stepped inside the same living rooms. Both were a generation older than the young people they photographed and wrote about. Both must have had a way of making themselves invisible in these spaces. A fragment from "Slouching Towards Bethlehem" could well be transposed as a Gedney caption:

> It is three o'clock and Deadeye is in bed. Somebody else is asleep on the living-room couch, and a girl is sleeping on the floor beneath a poster of Allen Ginsberg, and there are a couple of girls in pajamas making instant coffee. One of the girls introduces me to the friend on the couch, who extends one arm but does not get up because he is naked.

But Gedney's pictures didn't require words (nor did Didion's essay require pictures). In his notebooks, Gedney characterized *A Time of Youth* as "an attempt at visual literature, modeled after the novel form." The narrative of the book unfolds entirely through the photographs, with recurring characters that evolve and are changed, even if their transformations are not outwardly, explicitly revealed.

Organized in seven movements, the book's structure is also inherently musical, influenced by Gedney's avid appreciation for twentieth-century composers—Karlheinz Stockhausen, Roger Sessions, and especially Charles Ives among them. Music becomes a motif: the recurring appearance of the guitar in the first movement, a wooden recorder in the next. We wake up inside a crowded communal room, with two shadowy, androgynous-looking people, lying on the floor in a rumpled blanket, one cradling the other's face as he reaches idly for a guitar propped in the corner.

"Youth restlessly lounging over parked cars, in doorways, against store windows, garbage cans, parking meters, trees, each other," Gedney writes in his notebook. We are drawn to the infinite and unconscious arrangements of bodies, curled up against each other but gazing outward and away; bodies sleeping under tables; hands snaking around waists, kissing, hugging, hands clasping hands; or of clusters of bodies, drinking tea on mattresses in front of portraits of Jean Harlow and Marlon Brando, or playing guitar in stairwells and slouching on stoops. Many of the pictures were made inside a communal house called "the Pad," near the Grateful Dead's house. And the concluding sequence of the book takes place at a Human Be-In at Golden Gate Park. Twenty thousand people showed up but Gedney sought out individuals: a couple lying on the grass in deep conversation, a boy draped in beads staring defiantly at the camera, and another, eyes downcast, holding himself tightly close. In the final image, a lone man in the foreground hunches his shoulders, looking on as blurred figures wander off into the fog. With his hair cut short and in a dress shirt, the observer is an outsider in this world, a proxy for the photographer himself.

In the last months of Gedney's life, Joseph Caldwell recalls in his memoir, he only occasionally mentioned the books that came close to publication but were never realized—a deluxe edition of his India work, a book of his series of portraits of composers. "Could he have become so discouraged by these disappointments that he suffered a photographer's version of writer's block?" Caldwell writes. And yet: "Even though he had no instinct for self-promotion, he did have—I don't doubt—a sure sense of his own worth and the artistic value of the work he'd done."

The overdue arrival of this Gedney book is also a testament to the artist's faith in the longevity of his work and the degree of sacrifice he undertook to protect it. Often, I walk past Gedney's old apartment in Clinton Hill, Brooklyn, and look up at the window from which he made a daily series of the same photograph of the view outside: the elevated train that ran along Myrtle Avenue in those years, the shops and street below, and I think of the long, cold winters he spent working there, of his pictures of the street blanketed in snow.

Originally published on Aperture.org on June 29, 2021.

    WILLIAM GEDNEY'S RESTLESS YOUTH

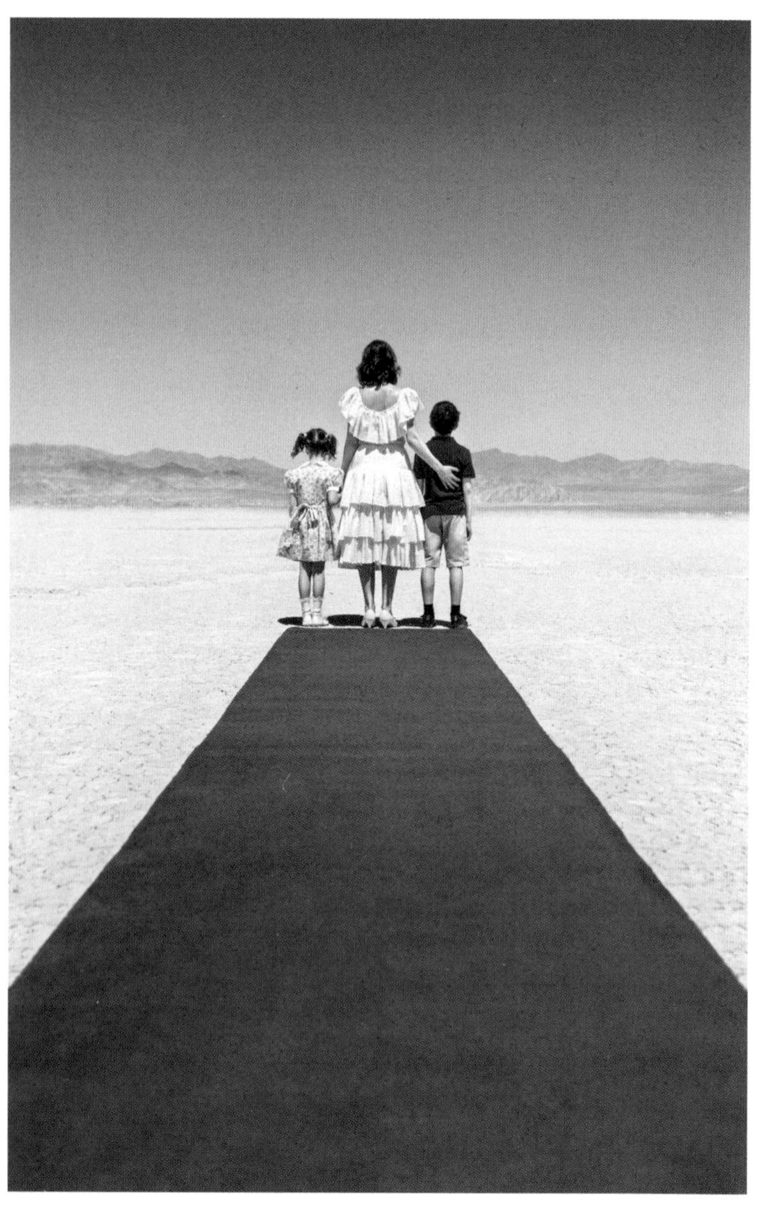

Diana Markosian, *Arrival in America, 1996*, from the series *Santa Barbara*, 2018

A Brightness I Had Never Seen: Diana Markosian in Santa Barbara

In October 1996, the Armenian American photographer Diana Markosian was seven years old, living with her family in Moscow, when her mother told her and her brother to pack their things; they were going on a trip. She didn't say where. "We left immediately," Markosian told me recently, "without even saying goodbye to our father." They landed in a new world that felt completely foreign but eerily familiar, too, almost as if it had been imprinted on her dreams.

"I remember the sunlight streaming through the windows," Markosian said. "All the palm trees. We walked through the airport, and everyone was smiling and wearing Disney hats, and shorts and sneakers, and eating hamburgers. My mother wore a white eyelet dress, and she was holding a picture of this older man. I'd never seen her so anxious before." A real-life version of the man in the picture approached, also smiling. Markosian, whose first name is pronounced *Dee-ahn-ah*, didn't speak any English, but she understood that he seemed to know her mother and that he was offering the children orange juice.

They had arrived in Santa Barbara, California, a place that, particularly for people living in post-Soviet Russia in the 1990s, symbolized a fairy tale. "Everyone knew *Santa Barbara*, no matter who you were," Markosian told me of her early childhood, spent in between Moscow and Yerevan, Armenia. The daytime series, named for the city where its three feuding fictional families lived, was the first American soap opera to be broadcast on Russian television. *Santa Barbara*'s often bizarre and humorous touches didn't always hold with American audiences, but in Russia, where it debuted in January 1992, its pop fantasy, dubbed in Russian, delivered a timely distraction from the recent collapse of the economy and the grim atmosphere that fell over the country.

Santa Barbara was a "national obsession of borderline-insane magnitude," the Saint Petersburg–born novelist Mikhail Iossel wrote, in 2017, in *Foreign Policy*. According to Iossel, its title became shorthand for melodramatic behavior: "'Oh, I can't stand those two, with their endless Santa Barbara!'" Russians hurried home for its broadcasts; they named their cats and dogs Mason, Eden, and Cruz after characters on the show. Graffiti appeared on buildings: "Santa Barbara Forevah!" The show was the total antithesis of Russia at the time—sunny, wealthy, vapid, glamorous, and, above all, free. *Santa Barbara*'s run lasted about ten years in Russia, nearly paralleling Boris Yeltsin's presidential term. Even today, the name is nostalgically embedded in the landscape—there is a Santa Barbara hotel in Crimea, for instance, with California-inspired architecture, and a Santa Barbara nightclub in Saint Petersburg, where, according to one travel site, clubgoers can find "the atmosphere of a permanent holiday."

Markosian's parents had degrees in economics and planned to become professors; in the Yeltsin years, they found themselves sewing and selling Barbie doll clothes to pay their bills. The children would leave the family's studio apartment at five in the morning to collect recyclable bottles for money. "We were desperate," Markosian said. At night, they watched television on whichever of their three temperamental sets happened to work. "Yeltsin came on nearly every evening, talking about the future of Russia, and everyone would tune in, because at any moment, *Santa Barbara* might come on," Markosian said. "*Santa Barbara* was our window on what we believed American life to be."

The man at the Santa Barbara airport, whose name was Eli,

     A BRIGHTNESS I HAD NEVER SEEN

drove them down streets lined with palm trees to a house that Markosian perceived to have "endless rooms." That first night, she woke to hear her mother crying in the bathroom. "She just kept saying, 'I can't, I can't,'" Markosian remembers. "Back home, she had been betrayed by the person who she had loved the most." In Russia, after Markosian's father had an affair and generally neglected the family, her mother, Svetlana, took out ads in newspaper classifieds sections for mail-order brides, exchanging letters with a few of the men who responded. That's how they had come to America. "I'm not going back," her brother, David, then eleven, told their mother on their first night in the States. "There was the feeling that this was never in the cards for us, and yet we had made it," Markosian told me. "That first year felt like magic."

It's a reimagining of that initial year in California that is the focus of Markosian's mesmerizing and deeply layered project, also titled *Santa Barbara* (2018), which includes both photographs and a film made with a cast of actors and a production crew. I spoke with Markosian in July, during a week when reports of Immigration and Customs Enforcement raids and the forced separation of immigrant families at the US-Mexico border dominated the news. When she began envisioning the project, after the 2016 US elections, she knew her mother would be the protagonist in the narrative. "This wasn't my story," Markosian said. "I didn't make the decision. I was just a little girl, following her footsteps at the airport—and now trying to understand her and the sacrifice she made for us."

As the project took shape, *Santa Barbara* the show emerged as a natural lens through which to view Svetlana's experience. In one of Markosian's most trenchant pictures, a red carpet unfurls across the desert, and Svetlana, in her white eyelet dress, clutches the hands of her children, alone together on the cusp of an empty and desolate world. "After years of watching *Santa Barbara*, she couldn't believe this was it," Markosian said. "That there was not much culture beyond the beach. She had such hope, and found nothing for herself."

Early on, Markosian drafted an episode-length screenplay. "I knew that this wasn't simply a project about photography, but was about storytelling," she said. The photographer Doug DuBois, a mentor of Markosian's, asked her, "Wait, you have a script, and you're not going to film it?" "So I found myself auditioning actors for eight months," Markosian recalled. She worked with Hollywood casting director Eyde Belasco, who had recently cast the 2018 film *Sorry to Bother You*. When finalizing her script, Markosian consulted Lynda Myles, one of *Santa Barbara*'s longtime scriptwriters. "I didn't want it to be a parody of the soap opera," Markosian said, "but I wanted to convey the idea of the shared experience of a story."

Photographs of the script, marked up with Myles's notes, and a copy of a "show bible" for the writers are part of the project's metafictional aspect, its conscious questioning of what it means to assemble and take possession of a story, whether the fictional universe of the show or the questioning and reimagining of a lived experience. Markosian's *Santa Barbara* includes staged photographs, the film, and archival materials—classifieds like the ones Svetlana advertised in, promotions for the soap opera.

Markosian added photographs and videos of casting calls for the eighty actors she auditioned for the role of Eli and the 263 who read for Svetlana, along with handwritten letters she asked the would-be Elis to write. The casting pictures are portraits of desire—evident in the faces of the actors are variations on longing, dreaming, and survival. "I'd ask them, 'Who is Svetlana?' 'She's a mother first, looking for a better future.' 'Who is Eli?' I'd say. 'He's a lonely man, looking for a fantasy.'"

Several months into the process, the original actress playing Svetlana quit. "It felt like my actual mother died," said Markosian. Devastated, she posted ads in Russia, Georgia, and Armenia, eventually casting a thirty-year-old Georgian actress, Ana Imnadze. "I brought her here and watched her experience the United States for the first time."

The staged photographs of Imnadze have a surreal and lucid quality of suspended disbelief, unshaken from the dream of the

     A BRIGHTNESS I HAD NEVER SEEN

soap opera. In them, Diana and David and Svetlana are led by Eli into a sun-drenched and bewildering existence of Halloween and Disneyland, going to the beach and eating at restaurants, buying the Barbies and Legos they'd never owned before. "At first," Markosian said, "Eli made my mother feel like a queen."

Over the course of production and photography, cast members began to explain Markosian's own family back to her. "Ana's face completely changes when she becomes my mother," she said. In the photographs, the Santa Barbara light provides fleeting and sudden revelations, the conflicted range of expressions of a woman who has had to put herself in a frightening, demeaning situation in order to escape a similar one, a woman who has to pretend in order to survive and who, on some level, yearns to believe a version of the dream that convinced her to leave behind everything she'd known. "I'd ask Ana to pose a certain way and she'd say, 'No, Diana, it's not Svetlana,'" Markosian said. "The actor Gene Jones was at first reluctant to put on one of Eli's costumes. 'Jeans,' he said, disgusted. 'Really, Diana? You'd think he'd try harder.'"

Markosian's suburban Santa Barbara scenes and domestic interiors inhabit a spiritual realm similar to that of Larry Sultan's photographs of his Southern California parents in *Pictures from Home* (1982–91). Both series present keenly introspective approaches to depicting family. Eli reads the obituaries or watches *Judge Judy*; Svetlana stares vacantly from the sofa or into the bathroom mirror at her new, hardly recognizable self. Absent from these photographs is the sense of love or a shared life that Sultan's parents exhibited; the gulf between Eli and Svetlana is palpable in the pictures. "It adds a sense of melancholy," Erin O'Toole, the San Francisco Museum of Modern Art's associate curator of photography, who organized the institution's exhibition of *Santa Barbara*, told me. "Both Larry and Diana are looking at their family from the perspective of their parents, embodying them." Jim Goldberg, for whom Sultan was a mentor and friend, and who explores his own personal history in his 2016 photobook,

The Last Son, had recommended Markosian's project to the department. "There's this idea in both Sultan's and Markosian's work about how much the Hollywood or television ideal imprinted on people and affected what they thought they wanted out of their lives," O'Toole said.

In *Dad on Bed* (1984), from *Pictures from Home*, Irving Sultan sits on the edge of his bed, an expression of ennui crossing his face. "I look like a full-on lost soul and I look at the picture and I say 'That's not me!'" Sultan chastised his son. "'In fact you went even further," Larry corrected him. "You said, 'That's not me sitting on the bed, that's you sitting on the bed. That's a self-portrait.' And I thought that was right."

At twenty-nine, Markosian is not much younger than Svetlana was—thirty-five—when they came to America. A graduate of the Columbia University School of Journalism, Markosian has lived mostly out of a suitcase for years, traveling on magazine assignments around the world. When we first spoke, she was in Amsterdam, preparing for a trip to Cuba early the next morning; it was evident how similarly driven she and Svetlana are. "She's not very casual with her life," Markosian said of her mother, who, with her brother's help in those early years, applied for a visa, learned to drive, got a job selling men's ties at a department store, went to night school, and earned a second PhD. "Mail-order bride" is a bit of a misnomer—Svetlana was not obliged to wed Eli, but in order for them to remain in America, she did. Within a year of moving to America, she married him in a Las Vegas wedding.

"I had called him 'Father,'" said Markosian of Eli, as she had no contact with her own at the time. "But my mother had outgrown him, and I think he knew it. I realized it when we were going to move. We were sitting in the front seat of a U-Haul at a gas station, waiting on my mother, and I remember Eli looking out the window and saying, 'I'm so tired of this.' I said, 'Of what?' And he goes, 'Of everything.' And right then my mother bounded over, smiling and shouting, 'Let's go!' She was so full of life. It struck me suddenly: she was at the beginning of hers, and he was nearing the end of his."

They'd planned to stay at a hotel and move to San Francisco together, but Eli abruptly filed for divorce. "The man who had saved us when we were desperate had abandoned us," Markosian said. Her brother was already in college, but for a year, she and her mother lived in a women's shelter to save money.

Markosian hasn't seen Eli since she was fifteen. She is close with her mother and brother, who have been involved with the project since its inception. Her mother lived in Portland, Oregon, and ran her own accounting firm, before returning to Santa Barbara. When Markosian visits, she sometimes finds Svetlana doing Pilates, accompanied by reruns of *Santa Barbara*. "At times, I've been so angry at my mother," Markosian said. "But she understood that I needed to understand her. Still I'd yell, 'I just don't get you!' And she'd tell me, 'You don't have to *get* me, Diana, just love me.'"

Several years ago, Markosian reconnected with her biological father and made two series of photographs, *Mornings (With You)* (2016) and *Inventing My Father* (2013–14). He was living in the family's mostly unchanged apartment in Yerevan. "He had kept essentially a time capsule of our possessions from when we had gone missing," she recalled. "There was a photo-album, a clock we'd had on the wall. To me, these things felt like treasures." For *Santa Barbara*, she had wallpaper made according to an old family photograph.

When Markosian returns to Russia and Armenia this year, she plans to photograph flashbacks for the film as still images. "I am trying to re-create the light I remember as a kid," she said. "In Russia, it was always suffused with this feeling that it's not enough. Santa Barbara gave us hope for something more. When we got there, it was a brightness I had never seen, almost impossible to believe."

Originally published in *Aperture*, issue 233, "Family," Winter 2018.

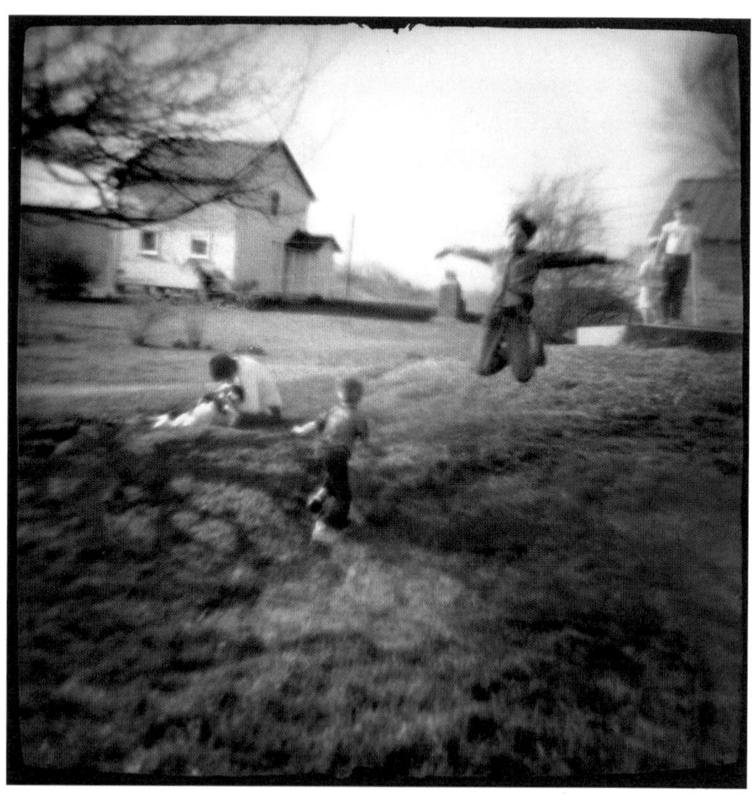

Nancy Rexroth, *Boys Flying, Amesville, Ohio*, 1976

Her Own Private Iowa

Vignetted monochromes of houses and yards tick by, as if seen from a train, or a moving car, each thick black frame like a window seal. Children in homemade costumes clamoring on front porches. Ghostly figures of boys suspended in midair. Solitary clapboard houses in bright, slanting sunshine with liquid-white exteriors. Pause on *Complexity*. Made in 1976 in Pomeroy, Ohio, its houses seem to palpably vibrate. If a group of turkeys is termed a "rafter," if a multiplicity of pigs is a "drift" (both animals are among the luminous-looking creatures in the photographer Nancy Rexroth's book *IOWA*), then a grouping of Rexroth's houses, flickering and starched white, might be called a "reverberation." More white houses, corralled in vines or partially eclipsed by shadows, both human and tree. The sight of children collapsed in a yard exhausted after playing put Rexroth in mind of photographs of the Battle of Gettysburg—"all those bodies strewn around," she told me recently. "It's also one of my pictures that I think of as deep Arbus."

They are photographs that feel at once timeless and long ago, strange and magic and familiar: look closely, and they trigger images submerged somewhere in your own past, partly imagined, as slippery and vivid as dreams. Rexroth spent the early 1970s roaming rural towns in Ohio and elsewhere with a Diana camera, making the pictures that would compose *IOWA*, published in 1977, and one of the most extraordinary photobooks of its era and since.

The title is an intentional misnomer. When she was growing up in Arlington, Virginia, Rexroth's family made summer trips to see relatives in Iowa, and the photographs she began to make in her twenties do not represent a literal place, but a portal, a feeling: the subconscious pull of memory. "It's as if it has always been there," Rexroth has written, "morphing away on the dark side of things, sad and joyful and filled with incredible longing." Only a handful of the photographs in *IOWA* were made in the state that shares its name.

The Diana camera was introduced to Rexroth by one of her MFA photography professors at Ohio State University, who had picked up Dianas for a dollar or two on a visit to New York's Chinatown. The Diana was plastic, prone to light leaks, and marketed as a toy. Rexroth took to it. "You can't get too serious about it," she says. "Every time you crank it to forward the film, it sounds like a ratchet, like a toy winding up. But I just used it like a camera. I never felt the need to say to people, 'Oh, I have this camera and it's very cute.' I would just go up and use it and never speak of it."

Still new to Ohio, the twentysomething photographer carried the Diana down remote roads she'd never traveled, knocking on strangers' doors, asking to be let in. A retired railroad worker in Logan let Rexroth photograph her bedroom: Rexroth's print depicts a floating abyss of snow-white space surrounded by the bed's dark frame. This was the first picture that would become *IOWA* — in all caps and italics on its stark lavender-pink cover, "larger than life" — using the settings of Ohio to stand in for the intense feeling she characterized as IOWA. There was a "pulse" Rexroth felt in certain towns. She would put herself in a state of mind she describes as a "daylight dream," on the days she went looking for IOWA. "You're a hunter, you get on your horse — your car — and you *pursue*," she tells me in one of our conversations. "I would turn it on like a lightbulb." After we hang up, I think: Of course, Nancy Rexroth setting out with her little toy camera named after the Roman goddess of the hunt, in pursuit of Mnemosyne, the Greek goddess of memory, mother of the muses!

Once in the 1970s, when Rexroth showed her pictures to the photographer Minor White, a founding editor of *Aperture* magazine, he asked her, "Why this camera? Why don't you just buy a Hasselblad and smear Vaseline on the lens?"

"The Diana is made for feelings," Rexroth wrote in *Aperture*'s fall 1974 issue, "The Snapshot." She might flick her hand over the shutter, to deliberately create blur. On one of the rare times when Rexroth returned to actual Iowa to photograph, she left her Diana cameras in the car, and they melted in the August sun, a plastic metaphor. She dispatched her boyfriend back home in Ohio to search in yard sales—he mailed her replacements.

Rexroth's material is real life, but she pulls from it like a short-story writer, subtracting all that is inessential. "I don't work sculpturally, from the ground up," Rexroth says. "I omit, I edit, I compose." When making *IOWA*, she did not allow signs or cars to enter the picture.

Her father's hometown in Iowa no longer exists. Many of the towns that Rexroth photographed in Ohio have also since disappeared. She continues to live and work in Ohio; recently her archives were acquired by the Cincinnati Art Museum.

In the same issue of *Aperture*, when Rexroth wrote that she sometimes made photographs with her eyes closed, she was telling a truth, just not the literal one. Rexroth tends to take numerous frames, moving in a dance, trying new compositions. It's the *people* in her pictures whose eyes are often closed or obscured. Think of the image of Rexroth's mother, blinking in delight as a sudden breeze lifts her hair skyward. Or Emmet Blackburn, a naive, retired widower whom Rexroth photographed on numerous occasions. Once, she accompanied him on a visit to his childhood home, which had been razed. Surely, here was a portrait of sorrow, that pulse of longing for a place to which one can never return. But near the spot where his house had been, Emmet proceeded to dance a jig.

Originally published in *Aperture*, issue 247, "Sleepwalking," Summer 2022, guest edited by Alec Soth.

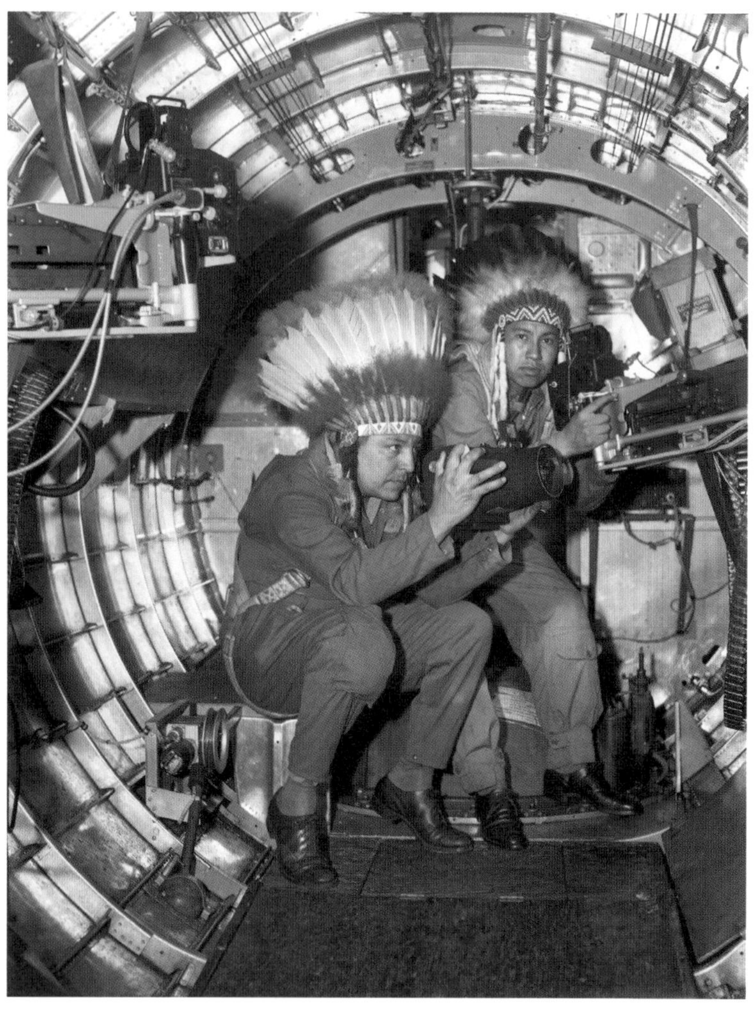

Horace Poolaw, Horace Poolaw (Kiowa), aerial photographer, and Gus Palmer (Kiowa), side gunner, inside a B-17 Flying Fortress. MacDill Field, Tampa, Florida, ca. 1944

I Want My People to Remember Themselves: Richard Throssel and Horace Poolaw

In an era when photographs of Native American people were largely made by outsiders, there is a portrait that acknowledges the act of its making. A photograph of Albert and Mary Lincoln, from sometime in the early 1900s, depicts a man, whose Apsáalooke (Crow) name was Thunder Iron, and his wife, Mary, seated beside him, both dressed magnificently. She wears an elk-tooth-studded dress. He wears a vest, gauntlets, and a belt with an intricately hand-beaded floral motif. They are posed against a white backdrop, but the framing reveals the improvised studio setup and exposes the patterned rug below their moccasins and a slice of wall. Thunder Iron's veneer is tough, his gaze is direct, his stance is fiercely protective. Mary keeps her hands folded in her lap, her eyebrows raised expectantly in an expression curiously close to trust. Together they form a picture that is at once frank and vulnerable, guiding the viewer to wonder about the person behind the camera.

Born in 1882 and raised in a small town in Washington State, Richard Throssel was of Manitoba Métis descent—Canadian, Cree, English, and Scottish. At twenty, seeking a drier climate for his rheumatism, he moved to the Crow Indian Reservation in south-central Montana, where he and his brother were hired as clerks by the Indian Health Service. Throssel arrived during the leadership of Plenty Coups, the last hereditary chief of the Crows, a warrior and visionary who went to great lengths to preserve the Crow language, culture, and lands threatened by US government initiatives, including the Dawes Act of 1887, which subdivided Native American communal tribal lands into allotments. One way Plenty Coups tried thwarting US land seizure was to invite new members into the tribe: Throssel was eventually adopted by the Crow and given his own allotment.

Throssel married the Indiana-born Florence Pifer, who taught him the Crow language, which she had learned while working as a teacher on the reservation. Around 1904 or 1905, the photographer Edward S. Curtis visited the Crow community while working on his ambitious project *The North American Indian*, a collection of photogravures and texts documenting Native American tribes throughout the United States, which would be published in twenty volumes from 1907 to 1930. He also made more than ten thousand wax cylinder recordings of tribal languages, music, and oral history.

Throssel, who had had sporadic art lessons, found Curtis's pictures to be "a revelation"; he traveled to visit Curtis in Seattle at his studio and was inspired by him to become a photographer.

Some of Throssel's early photographs—Pictorialist images of riders dramatically fording rivers, or close-up portraits of heroic warriors, such as the ones he made of his friend Chief Plenty Coups—reflect the Romantic influence of Curtis's style. In the early and mid-twentieth century, the photography of Native Americans tended to be propelled by the impetus either to promote a revisionist narrative, one of noble savages and well-meaning colonists, or to preserve the cultures colonists had aided in destroying. Curtis's project, bankrolled by J. P. Morgan, was a white photographer's attempt to document the "vanishing Indian" before he (women were less visible in Curtis's work) disappeared altogether. This meant there was no time to spare. Curtis traveled incessantly, relying on local assistants to do the groundwork and interviews with the people he photographed. By contrast, being part Cree and living among the Crow community, Throssel forged deeper, long-term connections. Members of the

          I WANT MY PEOPLE TO REMEMBER THEMSELVES

Northern Cheyenne tribe in southeastern Montana allowed him to photograph sacred ceremonies: in those images, elaborately masked dancers move through fields as part of the *Massaum*, or Animal Dance, a multiday dance that honored the healing relationships between animals and humans. Throssel's pictures are astonishingly surreal and dreamlike, the unique perspective of a near insider. They were so good that Curtis included a selection of them in the third book of his multivolume project.

But the work for which Throssel is most remembered occupies a more conflicted place between the white and Native American worlds. In 1909, he began producing several hundred plate-glass negatives, lantern slides, and a dozen moving pictures as part of a traveling government-run health campaign, led by Dr. Ferdinand Shoemaker of the Office of Indian Affairs, aimed at tampering twin outbreaks of tuberculosis and trachoma in "Indian" country. Shoemaker showed Throssel's images in well-attended lectures he gave to tribal communities all over the country. As the scholar Rebecca S. Wingo wrote, "It was a traveling lecture that left cultural devastation in its wake." Irony was unconsciously laced into these images; early colonists brought devastating disease to Native Americans and now the government was attempting to discourage traditional practices, such as sitting on the ground to eat, in the name of health. For one of the images meant to "correct" these behaviors, *Interior of the Best Indian Kitchen on the Crow Reservation* (1910), Throssel photographed a Crow family at a Euro-American-style dinner table. The elk tooth and beaded clothing of the mother and father contrasts with the china settings and strikingly patterned wallpaper.

"If the family were well-off agency employees themselves, it's possible they were in their own home," suggests Timothy McCleary, a professor at Little Big Horn College in Montana. "But even so, they wouldn't have worn their best clothes to an everyday dinner." Such styling lends a performative aspect to the photograph, casting the family as actors in an assimilation narrative, with subliminal suggestions of house and dress. Not only was this the way to eat, this was the way to live. Throssel, who received little credit for the work he did for this campaign, left the job out of frustration in 1911. He spent the last two decades of his life operating a commercial studio in Billings, Montana, returning to Crow lands to photograph the communities there, and served two terms as a state legislator, during which he advocated for Native American causes.

Although Throssel never became widely known in his lifetime, the scholar Peggy Albright's 1997 biography, *Crow Indian Photographer: The Work of Richard Throssel*, helped bring his pictures belatedly to light. And in 2003, the National Museum of the American Indian in New York held the exhibition *Telling a Crow Story: The Photographs of Richard Throssel*, seventy years after his sudden death in 1933. On the Crow Indian Reservation, Throssel's legacy has endured for decades through the studio portraits and candid pictures he made of women and children. The strength of his images resides in everyday, unguarded moments that feel inherently modern, freed from the dominant narrative of the "vanishing Indian" advanced by Curtis's vision. "Whether they were aware of the photographer's name or not, a lot of Crow people have been living with Throssel's pictures in their homes and in the community for years," says McCleary. "They become family treasures."

One of those ancestral connections reached the artist Wendy Red Star, who is Crow and first came across Throssel's portraits early in her career. In the late 2010s, when she began to source and incorporate materials from national archives into her photography-based work, she discovered an early-twentieth-century Throssel portrait of her great-great grandmother Her Dreams Are True (Julia Bad Boy, in English)—a picture she'd never seen before, a revelation.

*

Horace Poolaw, born in 1906, and working almost a full generation after Throssel, photographed his Kiowa community in and around Anadarko, Oklahoma. Like Throssel, Poolaw envisioned his legacy as something existing beyond himself. "I don't want to be remembered through my pictures; I want my people to remember themselves," Poolaw once said. It was a natural way of thinking for the son of a prominent local historian. His father, known as Kiowa George, was one of the keepers of the tribe's calendar — the pictographic record of the community's life, including notable events, ceremonies, births, and deaths.

At the core of the body of work Poolaw left behind at his death in 1984 are family and community pictures: his baby son Bryce, diapered and grinning on a sofa perched between his sister's two Anglo-looking baby dolls; his children Linda and Robert dressed as a cowgirl and a cowboy with toy guns. At regional Indian fairs and expositions and parades, Poolaw photographed veterans in procession and Kiowa beauty queens atop slicked-up convertibles. He photographed his son Jerry in his Navy years in a crackerjack uniform and a warbonnet. Poolaw also photographed Jerry at age five or six, in 1929, dressed in a tweed suit and hat. Tom Jones, cocurator of *For a Love of His People: The Photography of Horace Poolaw*, an exhibition organized in 2014 by the National Museum of the American Indian, rightly compares this image of Poolaw's to a portrait by August Sander.

Despite its undeniable power, Poolaw's work was not widely known outside his community for decades. "Whoever heard of an Indian who took Indian pictures?" his daughter Linda Poolaw said to me, half-jokingly, while speaking by phone from her home in Anadarko. In 1989, in cooperation with Stanford University, Linda codirected the Horace Poolaw Photography Project, which organized, printed, and archived some two thousand of her father's large-format negatives and launched a traveling exhibition. Although she maintains her father never intended to photograph "Kiowas in transition," his work is frequently understood as a document of the community's passage into midcentury American life. Poolaw's most productive years as a photographer overlapped with the two World Wars, the Great Depression, the rise of the automobile as an everyday fixture, and Franklin D. Roosevelt's "Indian New Deal," which aimed to reverse the forced cultural assimilation of Native Americans. Poolaw was born in a tipi and later moved into a modern house; his classmates at the largely white public school in Mountain View, Oklahoma, recall watching him and his brothers hitching up their horses before classes and galloping away after the last bell in a cloud of dust. He left school after the sixth grade and later apprenticed himself to two photographers who came through Oklahoma on the newly connected Chicago, Rock Island, and Pacific railroad lines.

He raised cattle, worked as a highway patrolman, and joined the Army Air Corps in his late thirties, teaching aerial photography at MacDill Field in Tampa, Florida. In 1992, a critic described Poolaw as "a witness to the tragic passing of the Kiowa world," a sentiment that reinforces the "vanishing Indian" trope of Throssel's era but sorely misses the spirit of these startlingly modern, at times ironic pictures, which transmit a sense of unfiltered joy.

"Out in the world, he was everybody's friend," Linda remembers. "We'd go to town and it was all 'Hi, Horace,' 'Hi, Horace.' He liked white people, Black people, Indian people, Mexican people, everybody." At home, Poolaw was strict and private. A stalwart Democrat, he read three newspapers a day; he disappeared into his un-air-conditioned darkroom for hours. "He didn't share that part of his life with us," Linda recalls, and even when her mother got a good job with the Riverside Indian School, he couldn't afford to print most of his pictures. "I think he was afraid to show them to people," she says. Over Christmas break in 1989, a group of Stanford students spread his prints over cafeteria tables in a tribal building in Oklahoma and asked members of the Kiowa community to help identify the people in them. Some cried, recognizing their relatives. At the culmination of printing and archiving in California, Linda drove her pickup truck to the beach and sat looking at the waves. It had been a year in which her father had become famous, as a result of the Stanford project, and compared to the greatest photographers of his time;

    I WANT MY PEOPLE TO REMEMBER THEMSELVES

a traveling exhibition would follow, and a portfolio in "Strong Hearts: Native American Visions and Voices," the Summer 1995 issue of *Aperture*. "I said to myself, I hope he's not pissed off that I'm doing all this!" she told me.

Poolaw used to tape pages torn from *Life* magazine outside his darkroom door. Today, it is difficult not to consider how his story might be different had his work been seen alongside that of his contemporaries who documented the social landscape of 1930s America for the Farm Security Administration. But unlike Walker Evans and Dorothea Lange, Poolaw did not focus on pictures of poverty, even when times were lean for his own family. Once, Linda asked her father why he photographed so many funerals. "Because everyone's all dressed up!" he said. Poolaw's grandson, John Poolaw, wrote in a text accompanying the 2014 exhibition that as a kid he was startled to come across a photograph by his grandfather that depicted his great-uncle Bruce and other family members dressed up in sharp suits, leaning against a shiny car. The image stood in stark contrast to the "sad and stiff " historical portrayals of Indians he was used to seeing: "I remember thinking that this photo should be titled 'fancy' because everything I saw in the photo exemplified what 'fancy' meant to me."

For a time Poolaw sold (and, more often, gave away) postcards printed with his images to tourists at bus stations and fairs. Stamped on the reverse of each was this imprint: "A Poolaw Photo, Pictures by an Indian, Horace M. Poolaw, Anadarko, Okla." While he proudly acknowledged his heritage, Poolaw also understood what it might signify to a potential non-Native buyer. His photographs of dances and parades tend to be made so closely that they deliver the feeling of being one of the participants. Occasionally, like Throssel, he pulls back to show the wider context for these events: a lineup of white tourists aiming their cameras at Kiowa dancers. Also, like Throssel, he was given permission to photograph certain ceremonies and moments normally off-limits to documentarians and tourists. In an image of a Peyote meeting, from around 1929, participants are lying on the ground outside a tipi, many turning their faces away from the camera. Among those standing is Lucy Nicolar, a Penobscot performer known by her stage name Princess Watahwaso, who would marry Poolaw's brother Bruce.

When she visited Oklahoma in the late 1920s, Princess Watahwaso helped usher in a new dimension to Poolaw's practice. Raised partly in Boston by a Harvard professor, she was a mezzo-soprano who made early records for Victor Records and worked as an entertainer in New York and for traveling shows; Bruce Poolaw had also joined the vaudeville circuit. No one in Anadarko had seen a woman like this, a glamorous, unconventional figure who rolled into town wearing jodhpurs and riding boots and smoking a cigar. The scholar Bunny McBride has written about how Princess Watahwaso knew how to play the "exotic Indian" while also challenging the expectations of her white audiences. Princess Watahwaso introduced the idea of staging to Poolaw, suggesting that more people might respond to his work if he took inspiration from popular films and vaudeville shows.

The element of performance in Poolaw's photographs allowed his subjects to have some control over their own images. They could show themselves as they felt they were or as they wanted to be seen. This is true of his field portraits of dancers wearing full regalia in ceremonies, or of couples donning their Western Sunday best. There are multiple photographs of his brother Bruce hamming it up in cowboy costumes and warbonnets, knowingly playing on the stereotypes he and Princess Watahwaso had learned to perform for white audiences who expected their own idea of Native authenticity. These pictures upend the colonial narrative and image record. The Indian did not vanish, but she could cut off her braids if she so desired. The warrior could ride a horse and drive a brand-new car.

Poolaw's photographs are revolutionary in their joyfulness and subversive in their embrace of change. In one of his masterful double portraits from around 1930, two Kiowa women stand in front of a tipi in near-identical, long-fringed leather dresses and beaded necklaces. The elder wears her hair in braids; the younger,

　　　　I WANT MY PEOPLE TO REMEMBER THEMSELVES

radically bobbed like Clara Bow, whose style was then being imitated all over the country. Poolaw's camera doesn't privilege the past over the present; it celebrates each equally. Photographs of his son in a Navy uniform and headdress—or of himself and a military gunner in their headdresses and flight suits playfully posing inside a B-17— seem to say, I'm wearing a warbonnet like the one my ancestors wore as they fought the country I'm now defending. Unlike you, I have the right to wear both uniforms. Unlike you, I can walk in both worlds.

Originally published in *Aperture*, issue 240, "Native America," Fall 2020, guest edited by Wendy Red Star.

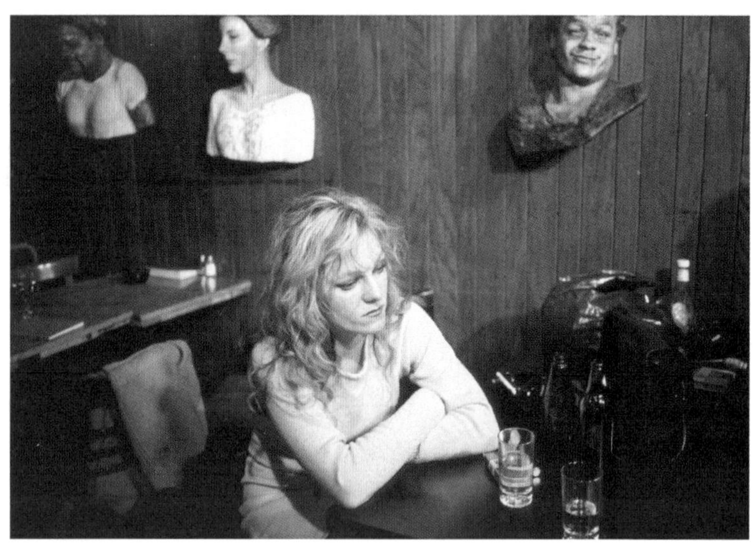

Nan Goldin, *Cookie at Tin Pan Alley, New York City*, 1983

Rewriting "The Ballad": A Conversation with Nan Goldin

Things were probably a little raucous, probably also a little reverent in those rooms, as soundtracks spliced from Maria Callas, the Velvet Underground, Screamin' Jay Hawkins, James Brown, and Yoko Ono played to a deeply personal visual diary of Nan Goldin's life, the late nights, the mornings after, the romance, and sex and drugs and violence. The first audiences mirrored the characters in the photographs, her closest friends and chosen family—downtown artists and actors and filmmakers and writers: Cookie Mueller and her girlfriend Sharon Niesp, David Armstrong, Suzanne Fletcher, among them, all calling out which pictures of themselves they liked best. The photos were made largely in the years before Goldin went into detox. It was also the height of the AIDS crisis; many of her subjects died young. "The book had become for me a volume of loss, a ballad of love," Goldin writes in the afterword to *The Ballad of Sexual Dependency*. Her color slides go straight into their bedrooms and before their bathroom mirrors, to the bars, to the street. As the title suggests, *The Ballad* feels musical in form, too, a narrative made up of distinct movements, heightening the division between men and women, which resonate in drastically different evocations of the same experiences, intimate and spontaneous. There are sections of women getting ready to go out, of men getting ready to go out, of women alone, of men alone, of women bruised and beaten, of men bruised and beaten, of women with guns, of men with guns, of women and men expressing what it is to be either and neither women and men, loving, living, dying.

At the heart of the story is the photographer, who points the camera at herself from the same unflinching vantage: "The photo of me battered is the central image of the *Ballad*," she writes. Goldin had been badly beaten by a lover, abuse that necessitated major surgery. That photograph is the hinge of the slideshow, of the book; it is also a visual echo of the loss of her sister, Barbara, who killed herself when she was eighteen and Goldin was eleven. Shortly after, Goldin was seduced by an older man, and it's that tension between pain, loss, and desire that propels her work. Terrified she too would die young, Goldin left home before the age of fifteen; eventually she moved to Provincetown, Massachusetts, where she became close to the drag scene; and to Boston, where she studied with the photographer Henry Horenstein, who turned her on to the work of Larry Clark; and to New York City, where the *Ballad* would take real shape. Now she lives between New York and Europe.

Since those early days, *The Ballad of Sexual Dependency* has been shown all over the world, the book reissued in multiple printings. This year it was on view again at the Whitney Museum of American Art, in the inaugural exhibition at the museum's new downtown home. On October 26, 2015, it was screened at Terminal 5 in Manhattan with live performances by Laurie Anderson and Martha Wainwright and other musicians, for Aperture's celebration of the thirtieth anniversary of the book's publication. When I called Goldin in New York, we talked about the evolution and constant re-editing of *Ballad*, the bar where she was working when she made it into the Whitney Biennial, and the relationship between photographs and memory in her work. It was a cold night. Goldin, who had been hosting friends for dinner, stepped out on her balcony to smoke and to talk. I found her to be as open and honest as her pictures.

                                    REWRITING "THE BALLAD"

Rebecca Bengal: I've seen *Ballad* as a book, I've seen it in a museum setting, I've seen it as a video, but I've never seen you, in a room, screening the slideshow. And in that sense none of us will have the complete experience of some of the early slideshows. So I'd like to talk a bit about all the different forms it's taken over the years and also how the slideshow itself has evolved.

Nan Goldin: You say it can't be seen in its early versions, which is interesting. But I actually found some recording tapes recently, though I haven't watched or listened to them. I made them on reel-to-reel tapes for years—the soundtracks. I have different versions of them. I tried different lengths of time. Sometimes it was an hour and a half, sometimes it was twenty minutes; until 1986 I had the drag queens in the middle, between the men and the women. And then a man named François Hébel wanted to show it in Arles, France, and he said, "What do you think about moving that section?" He was scared to ask—it is a bold thing to ask an artist to change their work—and I had quite a temper at that time. But I did it. And it was a really smart move on his part.

RB: One of the things that's so compelling about this work is that you're making it from within. This is the world that you were part of, and yet you were able to go outside enough in the way that an artist has to go outside to some extent, enough to be able to fully see. You were outside-inside. And those early shows, the ones I wish I could have seen, were often seen by the subjects themselves.

NG: Yes, the only people in those early audiences were people in the pictures. They were shown at a downtown space run by an amazing man named Rafik who is no longer with us. I think it's a place to buy film equipment now. But at the time there was a screening room and I would show it regularly there. I'd be holding the projector in my hands and the bulb would burn out and I'd run home and get another bulb. And the audience would wait. The slideshows were all really handmade.

I was just remembering the early black-and-white slides that were in the middle of the show then. They didn't really have a way to make black-and-white slides at the time, so they were very high contrast, really scratchy; they were very primitive and very personal. People would say, "Oh, I like that one of me." In a way that was what it was made for, so that people could tell me how they felt about it. They became part of it. I edited it *for* my friends. And sometimes friends who were living with me in the mid-'80s would help me edit it. Vivienne Dick, a Super 8 filmmaker, was a huge influence on my use of music.

RB: I read somewhere that one of the reasons you turned to slides is that it was cheaper, that you didn't have money for paper and darkroom supplies.

NG: No, that's not true. I started it when I was at art school in the '70s in Boston. I went to Provincetown and then I decided to spend a winter there. Basically I learned how to drink at art school; teachers at the school collected old cars and we'd sit in the cars and drink. But I learned how to print color. And I'm still friends with people I went to school with there. That was really art school.

I went to Provincetown and lived there through the winter. The way the school worked is that you would show your work three times a year and the teachers would grade it, or they'd give you advice or they'd say you were making shit. I had no access to a darkroom there, so that's when I started showing slides to the teachers. And a friend of mine would help me make the music. When I screened the slides at the famous "Times Square" exhibition in 1980, a boyfriend of mine was the DJ. So that was the very beginning of the slideshow. At first it was really just a series of pictures.

RB: You start taking pictures, and then you start taking more and more, and then they accumulate, and then eventually you start to shape the whole thing. When did you recognize that this was becoming a body of work? How did you arrive at this particular form?

   REWRITING "THE BALLAD"

NG: All I made were individual prints until 1978 except the ones I showed for credit. At my school, every year you'd hang your work in this huge armory in Boston as an installation, and if you won a prize you'd get money to travel. At that point I started making color prints and showing them on the wall, and I got the travel money and I went to London. There's a series a museum wants to buy—it's lots of skinheads that I was hanging out with then. The two months in London were some of the wildest times in my life. Literally. And I documented the whole thing. But I was always inside the work. It was never strangers. Even the skinheads. It wasn't like I went out looking for skinheads. I stayed with them briefly until they became the soldiers for the National Front. I witnessed that. In that period I lived a really wild life. Much wilder than anybody knows.

RB: It's a visual diary as you've described, but was that part of the initial impulse to photograph, as in, this wild time that's happening right now, this is going to disappear one day and photographing is my way of holding on to it?

NG: I talk about this a lot in the intro to the *Ballad* and it's true. It was *not* about the wild times. I never thought they would end. I was living in the moment, not documenting for the future. I think having an early death in my life, of my sister, made it more important to hold on to people. I'm aware even now that when I'm getting ready to leave a place, I photograph much more.

RB: At the same time you wrote that a photograph—

NG: That I thought it could save the person somehow. That I thought I could keep people alive. I really believed it until recently. I would light candles in churches too. I still do that. And I also thought I could preserve the memory of the person through a photograph. But without the voice, without the body, without the smell, without the laugh, it doesn't do much. Well, it keeps a memory, but then it becomes a memory of the picture at some point. It's important to understand when I took the pictures I was not thinking of their later use of preserving memory because I was in the moment—I didn't know what would be lost!

RB: You know Sally Mann in her memoir earlier this year said essentially the same thing—how photographs destroy actual memory. She was talking specifically about her friend, the painter Cy Twombly. She said the reason she remembers him so well is that she has so few pictures of him.

NG: Yes, I just did a text for my new book, *Diving for Pearls*— which is only out in German now, it will be out in English very soon—and I write about the difference between pearl diving and cultured pearls and I make an analogy between analog photography and digital photography. The pictures I took that came out all black, sometimes I remember those moments more strongly than I remember the ones that I photographed. It happened during some of the most important moments of my life, when the film came out black. I went to New Orleans for three weeks once with Cookie and Sharon and they were lovers at the time and they were breaking up. That was an incredibly wild three weeks and I photographed constantly. And I got thirty rolls of black film back. Except in the middle of one of the rolls there's a picture of Cookie looking in the mirror and putting on lipstick, and written next to her on the wall it says "Angel." It's the only picture that came out of these thirty rolls. And the camera worked perfectly before I went and it worked perfectly when I got back. It had to be voodoo.

RB: That's so haunted.

NG: And so my last statement in the book is, "Will voodoo ever work on digital photography?" The reason I call it *Diving for Pearls* is that David [Armstrong] used to say getting a good picture

     REWRITING "THE BALLAD"

is like diving for pearls. You take a thousand pictures to get a good one, like oysters with the rare pearl. It's true, and I used to say I'm not a good photographer. If anyone took as many pictures as I do, they'd be standing up here too. It's a lot to do with generosity, just taking thousands and thousands of pictures, and then where the art comes in is the editing.

RB: I think of them as distinct narrative forms: the individual pictures; the book; the slideshow, which is somewhere in between still photography and cinema. There's that word, *ballad*. It's a musical form in one sense, it's a literary form, and especially when you talk about photographs making their own memories, well, you're reshaping these memories all the time into new stories. Where does, say, the book fit in for you, in relation to the slideshow?

NG: It's a book of a film, and that's what it started as. Now it has its own life, and I love it. I want to make films; that's my life's dream. I haven't made that step yet, but I'm about to. I've found a collaborator and now I have to find a screenwriter. But that's all I've wanted to do since I was a kid and that's why I've never particularly cared about photography. That's why photography is easy for me to do. It's not as important to me to make great pictures as it is to make a great film, which has stopped me all these years. So this is my form of making movies. And Jim Jarmusch told me in the early '80s that he saw the slideshow as being a little bit like Chris Marker's film *La Jetée*, which is also made of stills. It's not really, because each slide is shown at the same time and it's not repeated. I mean, I would love to make something like *La Jetée*, but it's a lot more complex in the way that it uses the still.

RB: Who inspired you when you were a kid, when you first had the impulse to make films?

NG: I went to a hippie free school and we didn't have any classes. I mean, we once had a class in Italian — once, in four years; we once had a class in American expatriates in Paris, and once a class called "Ontogeny Recapitulates Phylogeny." We had school meetings every week, and that's where I learned to talk, which was very important for me. Because I was practically silent; I was so shy in those years. And then David and I went to the movies three times a week. So at fifteen I'd seen all of Antonioni, Jack Smith, Warhol, [Paul] Morrissey, Bertolucci, Bergman, John Waters (of course), Fellini, and all the American superstar women—all the Bette Davis, all the Joan Crawford, all the Jean Harlow, all the Greta Garbo. So that was my education—cinema, from the ages of fifteen to eighteen. And it still is. I wrote an article for *Cahiers du Cinéma*, they asked me to write about my favorite films. And I said that films taught me how to live. They taught me what relationships were. I learned everything I know from films.

RB: Jack Smith was at some of your early slideshows too, wasn't he?

NG: Yes, he and I did a screening together at Rafik's for Thanksgiving once. Things were very different back then. Artists hung out, we were all hanging out and very supportive of one another. And I remember the time the first person we knew went with a gallery and it was shocking to us. When I moved to New York in '78, I started with a gallery, Castelli Graphics, because Marvin Heiferman, who is a genius about many things but especially about photography—Marvin became my dealer for all of the '80s. In '85 he invited all these curators to Rafik's to come see my slideshow, and that's how it got into the Whitney Biennial.

RB: And what else were you doing at the time, apart from the world of the pictures?

NG: I was working as a bartender, at Tin Pan Alley, this tough bar on Times Square—back when it was Times Square, not Disney World—for this amazing woman who politicized me. This was Maggie Smith. I worked at the bar first, and then Kiki Smith

    REWRITING "THE BALLAD"

worked there, and Ulli Rimkus, who later opened Max Fish, and Cara Perlman and other female artists. There were a lot of street people, a lot of prostitutes and pimps and gang kids. Some of them really didn't like what happened to the bar. It was a neighborhood bar. Maggie cooked. It was on 49th Street and there was nowhere to eat. So people from CBS Records and all these places started coming because it was the only place with good food. And it was in this Japanese tourist guide, so suddenly a lot of Japanese tourists would come in, and the Clash would come in, and the bar changed and the regulars didn't really like it, having all these arty women working there.

RB: Well, the regulars never like a change.

NG: No, they don't. And there was a guy who'd come in and drink something like thirty Heinekens and pass out every day. I was doing the stills for a film. I used to do stills for downtown filmmakers like Bette Gordon and my work was at the Whitney, but I was still tending bar. One day I went back to the bar and that guy had gotten up and gone behind the bar and opened the wooden case where my cameras were stored and pissed on my cameras. And I screamed like an opera diva—you could hear me all over Manhattan—and I quit. That was my way out.

RB: That's incredible.

NG: It was. That bar really toughened me up. You know it was a lot of street prostitutes and their tricks, it was a lot of johns. Mostly they didn't even turn tricks, they would rob them and the johns would come into the bar just screaming. And the pimps always drank Hennessy and the prostitutes drank Long Island iced tea; they wanted to get as drunk as possible on one drink. That was a very tough life people were living, sex workers and all that. At a certain point I wanted out of the bar. I still dream about it. I still dream I have to get there at a certain time.

RB: How long did you work there?

NG: Five years. And in the first few years after my shift I would go to an after-hours bar and work there and it was a lot of bad cocaine, and when it closed at 9:00 or 10:00 in the morning, we'd go to breakfast and everyone would be reading the racing forms. That went on for years, and then I started working the day shift at the bar, and that's when I met the guy Brian who's in the pictures.

RB: That world is resonant in the pictures of *Ballad*, of course, but you just described another dimension of it so vividly. I'm curious, as time went on, what influenced some of the other changes you made in the sequencing of the slideshow. There are such distinct movements—the men, the women, the babies, the abuse, the sex, the moments of dark and light, of love and loss—that emerge throughout, and like you say, the editing of that narrative is so key.

NG: Maggie really politicized me. She is the one who helped me see the work is about gender politics. And I had talked to people in Provincetown about that in the '70s. After she became involved, I started making it more and more obviously political, to speak to her. Sometimes it was really hateful toward men and sometimes it was really positive, depending how I was feeling. Each showing was different. I made slideshows specifically for people too. I'd put in a lot of pictures specifically of that person and dedicate it to them. It could be anyone, a friend or a lover. In '83 I started traveling in Europe and showing it. I showed it many more times in Europe than in America. I showed it in European museums as one-off shows as early as 1983, and in underground cinemas and clubs all over Europe. It was accepted there earlier than it was in the US. One of the people who later became a lover of mine in Berlin, he raised his hand and said, "I'd like to be in the slideshow." And he was, afterward!

RB: Well, that's a pretty great come-on line. And given all those

                                         REWRITING "THE BALLAD"

versions, given its ever-evolving status, what is your relationship to *Ballad* now?

NG: I thought I'd stopped re-editing it by 1992; the last soundtrack was from 1987. But I re-edited it when the MoMA bought it in 2008, and they wanted it to be the same, they wanted it to be really dark—no pictures with light. Peter Galassi and his two assistants came down to watch as we were putting it together, and every picture that had light in it, he'd go, "No." But we put all those pictures in and they didn't notice, or they loved them anyway. We made one copy in 2008 for MoMA and one for a friend who's one of my biggest collectors in the world. We made that one much tougher, because he'd been a big part of the '70s and '80s at the Mudd Club, so we made it much more about that period. And this year I sold one to the Tate Modern and could not stop myself from editing a few categories in the analog version.

RB: That's what I keep coming back around to: the uniqueness of each slideshow, the uniqueness of what happened in the room each time you showed it, how it was all affected by where it was being shown and who was there, and what was going on all around, what it felt like. All the things I wish I could go back in time and experience—in that sense I suppose I really think of it as a performance.

NG: That's true. But then it became like Amy Winehouse. I felt such a strong connection with her because, you know, at the end I showed up at some fancy place in Chicago and I was too drugged to finish the slideshow, and there was a huge audience, and I know exactly how she felt when she showed up wherever it was and she couldn't perform. I mean, I had an audience of five hundred and she had an audience of probably fifty thousand, but it was the same feeling. And it happened to me twice. It's really painful. I loved that movie.

RB: I haven't seen it yet. I want to. I recently lost a friend who had dealt with some similar things, and I'll watch the film at some point. But there was a slideshow for this friend's wake, with music playing, pictures from these very wild, free, happier, beautiful times.

NG: Oh, that's good, it's good they showed those.

RB: I couldn't help but think of *Ballad* then, how it's a record of loss, but also of desire and love and light.

NG: Right. It can't only be the dark moments. There's a lot of light there too.

Originally published on Vogue.com on October 26, 2015.

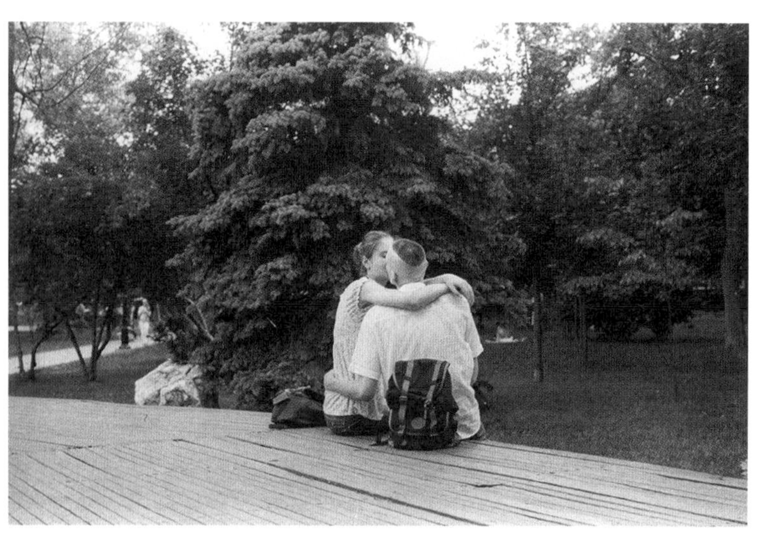

Yevgenia Belorusets, *Lucky Breaks*, 2018

Photography's Fiction of Truth: Yevgenia Belorusets and the Power of Ambiguity

Olga, a resident of Kyiv, is frightened by sunrises, prefers to be called by her full name, considers the patronymic form a kind of company, loathes the times when the city feels empty, and, when it stays that way too long, begins to "see what nobody sees and hear what nobody hears." She claims to perform acts of transformation—turning a pot of kasha into a hydrangea, a spoon into a blue ribbon, a postcard commemorating International Women's Day into a trio of matches. She swears this is all true. Depends, of course, on your definition of truth. This is one of the ideas at the heart of *Lucky Breaks* (2018), a collection of short fiction by the Kyiv-born photographer Yevgenia Belorusets, who intersperses the thirty-two brief stories, intermittently, subtly, with her documentary pictures.

Since the war broke out in Ukraine—the revolution of 2014, that is—another of Belorusets's characters has lost all sense of beginnings, and now wakes in the afternoon. This woman and her sister, a dishwasher at the American embassy, wear too-large clothes donated to them by Americans. The sister grows so bored of telling the siblings' story to the journalists, directors, and actors who come asking to hear that she starts replacing their narrative with the various traumas and misfortunes of their friends and neighbors, or with totally invented stories: "convoluted, complicated tales to force someone to really listen to what she was saying."

Many of the protagonists in *Lucky Breaks* may come off as eccentric, probably because they are isolated, which is also because they have been displaced. Most are women. They fled the Donbas region in eastern Ukraine, site of the conflicts of 2014, or they have to move away to earn a living, or their husbands are gone for months on end, also for work. The characters in the story "The Stars" finally begin to venture out of their basement shelters by charting the hours in which a newspaper column declares them astrologically safe—all clear for a Pisces to emerge between three and five in the afternoon, while a Scorpio is allowed out into the evening for a walk in a city "both smoky and bright." Even as long lines of "soiled and sullen" cars exit her city, the title character of the story "My Sister" is determined to stand her ground, no matter that she's almost all alone, surrounded by broken windowpanes and cords that snake in and out of other apartment windows—attempts to steal electricity by others who have refused to leave.

Snaking along, too, below the current of the subjects of the short stories of *Lucky Breaks* is a fugitive stream of black-and-white pictures made by the author. Belorusets, as translator Eugene Ostashevsky writes in an afterword to the 2022 US edition, came to writing from her life in photography, in which she uses "documentary methods," and she'd arrived at photography via a life in political and social activism. Her photographic series have focused on animals, brick-factory workers in west Ukraine, queer and trans families throughout the country, the residents of Roma settlements under attack by the far right, and protesters during the revolution of 2014, also known as the Revolution of Dignity. Russian special-ops and troops disguised as locals embedded in the fighting in the Donbas had turned the region into a surreal world in which notions of truth became increasingly murky—a fog of war that in the book Belorusets coats with photography.

Here and there in *Lucky Breaks* are pictures of abandoned-looking industrial buildings; a grinning, uniformed worker; persons sleeping in the grass. They are pulled, without identifying marks, from two of her documentary series: one, a project depicting people

PHOTOGRAPHY'S FICTION OF TRUTH

hanging out in parks—the dislocated feeling of leisure during wartime; the other, of the employees of a government-run coal mine who in 2015 and 2016 formed a protest to avert ecological disaster in their homeland, demanding that the mine's closure adhere to environmental standards.

None of this background is apparent in *Lucky Breaks*, whose themes already verge on the Gogolian absurd. Dislodged from their original context, thrown into the realm of fiction, her images add a semblance of authenticity—the "presence of the thing," as Roland Barthes put it, presumably assuring a more skeptical eye—in a place where reality has been upended. At the same time, her inclusion of the photographs plays on the reader's inherent desire for concrete evidence. At second glance, the picture asks more than it answers.

*

Lucky Breaks pushed Belorusets to look further into the unknown. In 2021, she published *Modern Animal*, her second book of fiction but her first published in English—a short, surreal novel told through diaristic accounts, fairy tales, and a series of lectures, some of which are delivered by animals. As in her photography, Belorusets had used documentary methods before she began to write, sometimes collaborating with her human interview subjects to transform the material of their conversations into fiction— "a kind of contemporary folk literature," according to one of her editors, Sebastian Clark, of the subscription-based imprint Isolarii. Like *Lucky Breaks*, *Modern Animal* includes some of Belorusets's photographs—the series *Zhyvy Kutochok (The Living Corner)* (2019–21) of chickens and cows on a farm, dogs, and birds of prey.

Shown in black and white, certain of her images—especially the closely depicted owls and hawks, and the sense of calm that seems to surround her cows and calves—aspire to the sensibility of Peter Hujar's magnificently secret and intimate photographs of animals. In one sense they are Belorusets's attempt to redress the hierarchical relationship of humans and animals taught in Soviet-style education—one in which schoolchildren learned to take care of plants and animals that were kept in a dark, small "living corner" of the classroom. "At that time, it was taught that the human being was the pinnacle of creation and animals were just tools," she said in an interview with *Palm*, the online magazine from the Paris museum Jeu de Paume.

"Pictures, if you think about it, are a kind of cage for animals," she continued. "In the book, text and images work in parallel. The photographs are not illustrative of the story, but arise from the same kind of interrogation." Her desire to photograph animals was grounded in her awareness of the fact that she would never be able to fully know them.

*

The English translation of *Lucky Breaks* was first published in the United States on March 1, 2022, five days after Russia invaded Ukraine. Belorusets has said that when she photographed and interviewed residents of the Donbas during wartime in 2014, she often felt like "a guest in a catastrophe," someone who had a home to return to. Photographing and writing short stories had prepared her for the events of February 24, 2022, only in the sense that, when Russia invaded Kyiv, as she wrote in her diary, "my body memory kicked in." That memory, coupled with shock, soon came to register as grief, and the recognition that the war was a continuation of the work she had already begun, as she also found herself doing things she had imagined for her fictional wartime characters. It gave *Lucky Breaks* an added layer of eeriness, although most of the eeriness of the book has to do with the cycles of historical time and myth embedded within the tales.

For the first forty-one days of war, Belorusets continued to keep a diary, which was published as a daily online dispatch and eventually collected as *In the Face of War* (which includes her photographs as well as works by historical artists such as Maria

Prymachenko and Tetyana Yablonska, and the contemporary artists Nikita Kadan and Lesia Khomenko), also published by Isolarii. Isolarii titles are designed as tiny volumes, the size of a small cell phone or a pocket hymnal. Each book, even one that amounts to 444 pages, as this one does, fits in the palm of your hand. You are conscious of the sensation of physically holding the first unsettling weeks of the war. In those days, Belorusets compulsively photographed, mostly in color, the things around her—perhaps the most common impulse in photography, to preserve the sense of something before it disappears altogether. She did it, she writes in an afterword, "to somehow interrupt the flow of this particular, unbearable story." And yet, she was caught in the position of preserving a story she herself had written, with uncanny, disorienting prescience.

*

With *Lucky Breaks*, Belorusets had been operating in the vein of others before her who have inserted photographs into literary texts, but especially W. G. Sebald, whose melancholic-cosmic novels of time, memory, and the aftermath of war—*Vertigo*, *The Emigrants*, *The Rings of Saturn*, and *Austerlitz*—famously interweave uncaptioned photographs within the twisting narratives that wander alongside their forever rambling protagonist as he falls into digressive encounters with strange fellow travelers, stepping into a great pool of time.

No one likes to be duped, but some people don't like to have a good time. Some of Sebald's critics, like all overly literal-minded readers, spend too much energy worrying about what stories and images he may or may not have borrowed or embellished, invented or not, which stories came from familiar photo albums and which came from unknown subjects of photographs sold by antique dealers—which is to miss out on the pleasures and lessons of his books. It is to miss the notes of comedy in his writing, and in the interplay between word and image.

In an essay for the *New Yorker* praising the too rarely observed humor in Sebald's work, the writer James Wood locates the comic in the photographs in the books, particularly in the "self-conscious antiquarianism" of Sebald's unnamed first-person narration: the existence of "an otherworldliness of the present. His very prose functions like an old, unidentified photograph." The haunting cover image of *Austerlitz*—an old photograph of a young boy in a field, wearing an outfit as aristocratic as those in a Rembrandt—could not be "of" Jacques Austerlitz, an invented character. But did the picture itself make it seem as if it could be? When Wood, examining the photograph in the author's archive, flipped it over, he found a junk dealer's penciled-in price: 30 pence. "Scandalously," Wood writes, "where documentary witness and fidelity is sacred, Sebald introduces the note of the unreliable." The greater issue, he proposes, is whether Sebald's use of that particular photograph implied a more direct connection to the historical events of the book.

Perhaps we're meant to question these things, and that's part of the point—not that Sebald was the sort of writer who had "a" point. For a writer such as Belorusets, whom I would call an indirect descendant of Sebald's, both photograph and story seem to gain power the *more* assiduously she calls their veracity into question. "Any document is partly a lie," Belorusets has said, "and this is especially true of documentary photography, which only ever conveys a small part of reality."

Like the found photographs of Sebald's novels, Belorusets's repurposing of her own pictures allows them to function as enigmas. Rather than illustrate, they suggest the feeling of a world. Rather than dutifully serve the plot, they tend to shift the attention elsewhere. In place of proof, they respond in dreamlike fragments, deliberately casting doubt. Sometimes her photographs misbehave, like punchlines. Reminiscent of the isolated, dream-spinning Silesian narrators of Olga Tokarczuk's *House of Day, House of Night*, the protagonist of Belorusets's "The Seer of Dreams" insists on her fantastic somnambulant visions of ancient Ukraine, of rivers of blood, of elephants wearing embroidered saddles.

                    PHOTOGRAPHY'S FICTION OF TRUTH

The seer's final divination of the story—of a prophetic, two-headed dog who forecasts images of prosperity and happiness—is instantly undercut by the mortal intrusion of Belorusets's own photograph, of what appears to be a miners' locker room, with shelves of rusted tools and hard hats and coffee mugs. Is this a joke on the dreamer or on the reader? Does it matter? Do we even have to ask?

Brooklyn, November 2022

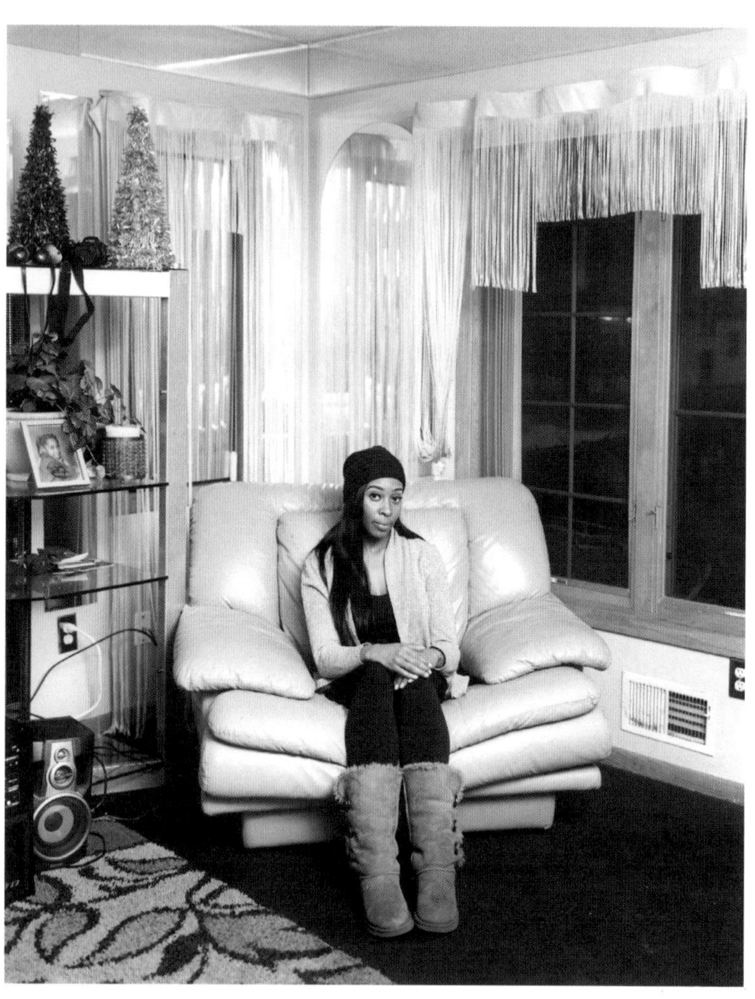

Alec Soth, Alda Reed, Logan Avenue, Minneapolis, 2018

In the Place Where Prince Lived

In Minneapolis, Prince was everywhere. He held impromptu, late-night shows at Paisley Park, his studio complex in Chanhassen, twenty miles away from the city, testing new songs on audiences that sometimes numbered only in the dozens. He rode his bicycle to the arboretum three miles west of Paisley; he would show up at the Caribou Coffee in Chanhassen and pay with a hundred-dollar bill, tipping the change, because his custom-made pants had no pockets. He might slip into a back booth at Bunker's on Sunday or Monday nights where his old New Power Generation band members Sonny Thompson and Michael Bland still perform. Sometimes he joined them onstage. When he was filming *Purple Rain*, he showed the director the storms of his hometown: "Clouds would begin to churn and roil," Albert Magnoli remembers. "Prince would grab me and take me outside." They stood in a field and watched as the sky changed from gray to purple.

"I like Hollywood," Prince once said. "I just like Minneapolis a little bit better." For all the houses he kept at various times, in Spain and in Toronto and in Los Angeles, he always returned to his hometown, where he made his best work. Thousands of unheard songs allegedly survive him in the archives of Paisley Park, but Prince left impressions everywhere he lived. Recently, the photographer Alec Soth and I went looking for them.

Plenty of Prince fans had set out on the same trail. It occurred to us that what we were doing was not all that different from Prince himself. As a Jehovah's Witness, encouraged by his faith to evangelize, he reportedly knocked on strangers' doors around Minneapolis and Chanhassen, sometimes as himself, often in disguise.

Neither of us had ever met Prince, but Alec had come close. In late 1985, Prince moved into a three-story yellow mansion on the land adjoining his family's house, a couple of miles from where Paisley Park would be built. The two places were separated by woods, fields, a little creek. Alec was fifteen and for at least a year he lived in the actual midst of Prince. "I would walk through the forests to the fence line, and watch his security patrol the place on snowmobiles," he told me as we drove. To live in such sheer proximity was to feel a little bit royal. And then, a year later, shortly after Alec's family moved into the city, they learned Prince had expanded his holdings, purchasing the property and demolishing the farmhouse that once stood there.

I didn't have anything that could top "Prince, my next-door neighbor, destroyed my childhood home." I did have a sharp, distinct memory of the first times I'd listened to Prince — "When Doves Cry," a thousand miles away from Minneapolis, a little kid in the backseat of the car traveling from the mountains to the beach, pressing my face into the window whisper-singing the lyrics, understanding only enough of them to hope that no one could hear the things I was thinking. As I stared out at a receding rural landscape, I had the distinct impression I'd just been handed a connection to a future self. Maybe that was the Prince bulldozer again, razing some corner of my childhood.

Two Aprils ago, I surfaced from the subway to a dozen texts flashing on my phone. In the shock of the news of his death I was struck by an immediate and urgent desire to hear Prince played out in the world, slipping out of teenagers' shared headphones on the subway, out of car radios and open windows, to reattach his music to the streets. Prince belonged everywhere, I thought, to everyone. The outpouring at the impromptu block gathering Spike Lee held outside his Brooklyn studio later that night was

                    IN THE PLACE WHERE PRINCE LIVED

cathartic: purple umbrellas, MTV News microphones, in the spirit of the crowds I'd later see videos of in Minneapolis outside First Avenue, the club Prince made famous in *Purple Rain*. Valiantly, everybody tried to hit the high notes together.

Miho Takayama was fifteen and growing up outside Tokyo when her mother took her to her first Prince concert. She didn't understand the lyrics, but even in Japanese, she didn't have the words yet to explain what Prince had awakened in her, or the magnetic pull she felt, something akin to the reverse of homesickness.

"Prince, *oh, my God!*" she told us. "That was it. I knew right then I was going to move to the city where he lived." She had family living all over the world, but Minneapolis felt totally foreign. "I pictured endless flat land with giant grocery stores," she said. "Every kind of cereal you could want." She thought for another minute. "And, of course, Prince."

Miho is now forty-two; she works as a waitress. When we visited her home in northeast Minneapolis, she was dressed in leggings and boots and a long hooded sweater she'd sewed herself. Prince never lived here, but amid her cacti collection and Thelonious Monk posters were her framed ticket stubs, the zines she brought from Japan, the sheet music for "Little Red Corvette." Her beloved dog, who had recently died, was named Oji — Prince, in Japanese. Prince is the reason for the guitars and amps in her living room. In the years before the deaths of both Princes, Miho had begun teaching herself to play the bass lines of his songs.

Twenty-two years ago, with two suitcases, a backpack full of Prince cassettes and VHS tapes, and a little money saved from a job working at Mister Donut in Japan, Miho made good on her promise to move to her idol's hometown. She scoured the *City Pages* listings, found a room in a former school that had been transformed into "a really junky house" with a full-size gym. One of her roommates, Victor, slept in a bed pushed onto a stage. When they told her how much the rent would be each month, she had to ask, "What is 'bucks'?"

With little spoken English she followed the music. One October night in 1996, when George Clinton was playing at First Avenue, it was obvious where the after-party would be. "I just went up to someone and asked them, 'Are you driving to Paisley Park and can I come along?'"

They drove the half hour into Chanhassen—"there was nothing out there then, no one," she said. "But when they let us inside Paisley Park, I saw George Clinton and Prince talking on a couch, and a little later, Prince got onstage. From then on, every decision I made was motivated by Prince."

She got a job; she bought a car to make the drive to Chanhassen at a moment's notice. In pre–cell phone days, she waited in the computer lab at the University of Minnesota until it closed at midnight, obsessively refreshing her screen: "You might not find out till, like, 11:57, and then you'd drive to Paisley and wait in your car till maybe 2:00, 3:00—whenever they came outside and told us it was time."

In the club room by the soundstage, Prince kept the lights low. There were no clocks, no windows. "Prince might play songs we never heard before; he might play forty-five minutes and that's it, or he'd come back and play again, or sometimes you'd look over and he's riding his bicycle all around the soundstage," Miho said. "There'd be people falling asleep in the booths. By the very end of the night, there were only a few of us. We'd walk outside at 6:00, 7:00 in the morning and the sun would be coming up and we'd just look at each other, like, Wow, we just saw Prince." She would drive straight to her catering job, with a sleepless stardust feeling, deliver coffee and pastries all over Minneapolis, nap a few hours, and, if the word came, drive out to Paisley Park again.

Over the years, the free nights at Paisley turned into $7 door charges, $10, $20, $30. Miho was one of just a few dozen guests on a night Prince performed for Madonna and her backup dancers. She has seen him play, she reckons, "hundreds of times." She hasn't been back to Paisley Park since April 17, 2016, the night Prince hosted his last DJ party, and showed the crowd a new custom purple Yamaha piano and a custom Gus guitar. "I tweeted to Prince right after: 'Ur new guitar and piano are lovely' and he retweeted it right away. It made my night—forever," she said.

On the front door of the white house with the pitched roof on the corner of Newton and Graham Avenues, *Keep Out* and *Beware of Dog* signs warned potential unwanted visitors, but there was no audible bark upon approach and a contractor next door claimed no one had been by in "a while." Prince lived here in his father's house off and on as a teenager; now the house is in his sister Tyka Nelson's name. Arrangements of purple silk flowers lined the porch and front walk; out back, an air freshener with Prince's Love Symbol hung from the rearview mirror of an SUV.

Across the street, a woman chided her preschool-age son for eating dirty snow. She glanced at Alec setting up his camera on the street, and looked back at her kid. "Maybe one day *you'll* grow up to be so famous someone will come take pictures of our house," she said.

Three white company cars were parked in front of the multi-color brick house on Russell Avenue, each bearing the name of a cleaning service called Heaven Scent. The owner, Robin Crockett, was unloading groceries in the driveway. She didn't seem all that surprised to see us. "Oh, just another day in the life of a human being!" she said breezily when I asked how she was doing. It was her first day off in two weeks and she wasn't expecting company, let alone a couple of strangers off the street. "Come on in," she said.

She handed off bags to her youngest, sixteen-year-old Daisha, directing her where to put everything. Robin was her business's own best advertisement—warm yet formidable, spotless and efficient. The cream-color carpets in her house were plush and so immaculately vacuumed that even our sock feet undoubtedly left an impression.

"I've had people here from all over the world," she told us. "Reporters, news crews at first, but fans too. They'll start crying on our steps. There's this lady who comes and says she knew him. She just wants to sit in the yard sometimes. She seems genuine about how she feels—she just wants to be in the general space. Around June 7, his birthday, people will bring flowers. I'm used to that now."

When she came back to north Minneapolis to look at the house, she didn't recognize the address at first from its realtor listing. "When we were teenagers, we didn't know it by the house number," she said. "We just knew it was the Anderson house. We could close our eyes and find it by following the music." They used the side door, heading straight for the basement, where a teenage Prince Rogers Nelson would be jamming with his best friends, André Anderson, now known as André Cymone, and Morris Day, in their early bands Grand Central and Shampayne (also spelled Champagne). They played one of their first paying gigs at a church around the corner, for which they each earned $3. When Prince was kicked out of his father's house, Mrs. Anderson, who had six kids of her own, took him in. "Prince was already so focused, so serious," Robin said. "He could go really deep and then he'd hit those high notes. Our friends called him 'Gazoo,' like from the *Flintstones*, 'cause he'd wear this white space suit–type suit, bell-bottoms, and high-heel platforms—and then he had this big Afro." Prince wears his Gazoo look in a photograph from that era, the members of Grand Central standing in what is now Robin's front yard, holding up large letters that spell out the band's name.

"You see down the street?" She pointed through her kitchen window. "We would sit on that corner there on Plymouth in our pink foam hair curlers and wait for the go-ahead so we could come over and be groupies and watch them practice. It was OK to be a groupie! It was part of our culture. We were North-Siders and so were they."

When Robin bought the house in 2007, she moved her middle daughter, the rap artist BdotCroc, into the basement where Prince had slept: "I wanted her to have a hangout, a kick-it area where she could have her friends over like we did." Prince had spent his allowance to decorate his makeshift bedroom with mirrors, posters of Jimi Hendrix, a swatch of white rabbit fur. In heavy rains, it flooded. "He had to walk on concrete bricks," Robin said. "But he'd sit down there and play guitar for hours." She led us into the unfinished area: laundry and exercise machines. "This whole space was drums, all their stuff. This basement had a lot going on. This is it. This is where greatness came from."

We didn't get to visit inside the white wooden house on North Arm Drive, where Prince eight-tracked "Baby, Baby, Baby." This was sometime around 1978, the year stamped on the back of some snapshots discovered in his vault after his death—an early self-directed photo shoot. In one of these, which would become the cover of his unfinished memoir *The Beautiful Ones*, Prince stands before a lattice-print wallpaper, holds a camera to the side of his face, an early selfie. *I took this picture of the heater and I in the bathroom mirror*, he writes in cursive on the reverse. *(Sorry!)* In other shots, he puts a knee-high-boot-clad foot to the sink, a fake prop hand alternately emerging from the pocket of a hoodie, or poking out of his cut-offs.

When we drove up to the house by Lake Riley, the driveway where Prince practiced motorcycle laps for *Purple Rain* was covered in mud; fresh insulation wrapped a building under construction. Prince was twenty-two when he moved into the cream-color house on Kiowa Trail. Immediately, he had it repainted purple and installed a sixteen-track studio where he recorded parts of *Purple Rain*, *Controversy*, and *1999*. The original Purple House was reportedly razed two years after Prince's father died in 2001, another childhood home destroyed.

A delivery guy in a purple hoodie slowed down when he saw the camera, cracked the window of his Honda. "I heard the people who bought it live right down the street," he said. "They wrote Prince a letter saying they wanted to buy it." At least, he pointed out, the new owners had kept the original gates, with the sculpted heart and the simulation of a peace sign.

Not everyone wanted a picture. On the shores of North Arm Lake, where Prince rented a waterfront house from 1979 to 1980, the current owner stepped away from his remodeling but didn't invite us in. "We're renovating," he said. "Maybe you can come back when we're done."

He reckoned that was still several months off, introduced himself as Brian Giraud, originally from Canada. "I used to be a videotape editor for one of the stations up there," Brian said. "I worked with him once. I worked with Bowie, all kinds of people. Kenny Rogers . . ."

I asked who had been his favorite.

"Oh, probably Billy Joel," he answered mildly. We were standing on Prince's long-ago back porch, overlooking the iced-over lake. I said I'd heard that Prince recorded *Dirty Mind* in this house. A valentine-red hot tub was visible from beneath a sheet of thick plastic on the sunporch; he nodded in its direction. "Now that, I think, is from when he lived here."

At night, Paisley Park glows purple, but in the daytime, the sixty-five-thousand-square-foot complex camouflages into its habitat, the Chanhassen suburbs of office parks and strip malls that have grown up around it. A General Mills factory is down the street. Bret Thoeny, the architect commissioned to design an artist's compound where Prince could record albums, make movies, rehearse world tours, and house his fashion designer's atelier, found the site in the mid-'80s, almost by accident.

"It was spacious and level and green," he said on a recent morning from his office in Los Angeles. "There were all these beehives—someone was raising bees. It was really rural out there. We essentially gave him a blank canvas: a white metal building on a green landscape. You could project any color on it. The pyramid roof, that was his idea."

Graceland Holdings now manages Paisley Park, which is under stricter rules than Elvis Presley's house—no cell phones, no cameras. "But Paisley was never like Graceland," Thoeny said.

It wasn't a house, for one. After Prince's *Lovesexy*, some of the first albums made at Paisley were by other artists—Madonna's *Like a Prayer*, Paula Abdul's *Forever Your Girl*. "Prince actually followed George Lucas's vision. After *Star Wars*, Lucas didn't want to have anything to do with Hollywood. He made everyone come to him." The architect would make 3-D scale models of Paisley Park; he'd fly them to wherever Prince happened to be performing and carry them backstage.

One of the first things you see on a tour of Paisley Park is Paisley Park itself, a miniature replica of the building displayed in the atrium by the Little Kitchen, where Prince used to make omelets. This scale model is actually an urn, and Prince's cremated ashes are housed inside. It was made at the request of the Nelson family by the company Foreverence, which has also made custom urns for Lemmy Kilmister of Motörhead (in the shape of a black hat) and Bob Casale of Devo (an energy dome).

"Lots of people walk in and start to cry right away—it's very emotional," our guide, Mitch Maguire, told us. Above were tall skylit ceilings, walls decorated with an *Around the World in a Day*–esque blue sky and clouds. Painted butterflies trailed down a wall. Audible from an adjacent landing were three white doves—not crying, or even cooing, but jostling about in their large cage. "Those are Divinity and Majesty," Mitch said. "And there's the original Divinity too."

Many pains had been taken to leave verisimilar traces of Prince—a hat sitting on a piano in Studio B, allegedly where he had left it; fake candles to mimic the real ones he kept burning everywhere, at the same height at which he'd left them. But you could sense Prince most palpably in the clothes on display, the exquisite custom suit for *Under the Cherry Moon*, the safety-pinned denim jacket, all the studded shoulders, all so precisely tailored, so physically small, so human. The Ping-Pong table in Studio B was a testament to his legendary prowess in the sport. You could sense Prince, the consummate worker, in the framed letter of emancipation, handwritten on wide-ruled notebook paper, that he sent to Warner Bros. Records—uncompromising but also as heartfelt as the letters and diary entries that people still leave for him here or tuck into the mailbox at the house on Snelling Avenue where *Purple Rain* was filmed. Alec photographed one of these, an entry illustrated with pencil-drawn hearts and a star sticker, preserved from the very Prince year of 1999: *I'm still in love with prince and i still want him. It all I think about. Why can't I just have him, it all I want... I Will Always <3 Prince Forever!*

Prince's Super Bowl performance was projected on the gift shop walls but none of his music was sold there. "We tell people to go to Electric Fetus," a cashier said. She looked flustered and maybe a little pained when I asked. I instantly felt bad—after all, she was a fan too. Electric Fetus was Prince's favorite local record store, in business since his childhood. "We're figuring it out," she said. "This is still new."

In the NPG Music Club Room, where we were invited to take a seat on the plush purple couches, you could again sense Prince, the cosmic genius performer. The ceilings soared, but the room felt small and intimate and it was nearly as dark as Miho had described. Above us was a screen where Prince sometimes projected movies during his performances—*Finding Nemo* was a favorite. The stage was maybe fifty feet away.

"You didn't look straight at him, but you always knew he was there before you saw him," Miho had told us. "Sometimes he'd be standing right behind me. He wore perfume, oils. He always smelled so good. And then he would disappear."

Before he got a job at Paisley, our tour guide Mitch went to Prince's impromptu shows there too. He didn't remember seeing anyone like Miho, nor, when I asked her later, did she recall seeing anyone like him. I didn't doubt either of their stories, but I did understand how, on those nights, each of them would not have noticed the other, how their admiration for Prince surpassed all else. Until the night ended and the doors opened onto a Chanhassen morning, you might not be aware of any of the few dozen other people in the room with you, only Prince and his perfume.

                    IN THE PLACE WHERE PRINCE LIVED

Just east of Paisley Park, and along Highway 5 is the memorial fence, where fans still leave zip-tied drawings and umbrellas and charms and purple teddy bears and, mysteriously, a purple spatula. They write letters to Prince, delivered in plastic sandwich bags filled with butterfly decals. They tell them how much he changed their lives, how he made them feel special. *Dear Prince, I learned to eat light because of you. Dear Prince, I see all the signs that you saw me.*

Picture Prince riding his bicycle past Paisley and the fence and over the creek and through the tunnel below the highway, where hundreds of graffiti tributes and paintings now cover the walls; so much purple spray paint. It would have taken him maybe ten minutes to ride along the sidewalks, past a pair of wooden bird feeders and red sumac growing on the roadside, and find himself in another forest, surrounded by open fields and tall grasses and more sumac and roaming deer.

One day he was the outsider, wandering through a series of walking trails on the other side of the highway. "Who are you?" a man asked him.

"I'm Prince," said Prince.

"Prince of what?" the man asked, a question that must have delighted his visitor.

This is a story told by Leslie, a volunteer guide at the Temple of Eck, which opened in Chanhassen in 1990, three years after Paisley Park, across the highway. Its gold ziggurat roof mirrors Prince's pyramids: ancient Sumer in a highway conversation with ancient Egypt. Eckankar evolved from the Punjabi Sant Mat tradition, which believes that the universe was created by a series of sound waves, emanating from a divine spirit.

The Eckists, Leslie explained as she walked us through the octagonal classrooms, believe in dreams and past lives and in what they call soul travel, which they say is achieved partly through the singing of the HU—a repeated, simple chant, just that sound. The living Eck master is a thin, balding Wisconsin-born man named Harold Klemp; he is frequently depicted in glasses and an ordinary suit. Portraits of Harold fill the rooms of the temple, in paintings created by Eckists: Harold in the cosmos, Harold with a chrysalis, Harold looking like a tax accountant, Harold looking a little like Merle Haggard. I asked Leslie if Harold lived here too. "He doesn't," she said, a bit mysteriously. "But you just may have an encounter with him around town." As we headed back into Chanhassen we popped one of the free Eckankar CDs into the car stereo. The voice of Harold patiently explained the concept of soul travel in a distinctly Midwestern accent: "on the road," he intoned, in drawn-out *o*'s, "to home."

The steps that once led to the farmhouse where Alec grew up are still there. A large visible hole in the ground marks the place where his house used to be, a cavernous impression in the ground. As we approached, a family of deer froze and then fled through the forest, in the direction of Prince's place.

On the land next door there is now another hole in the ground—the yellow house was demolished, too, after Prince moved out for good. Back here, probably a quarter mile from the road, the air was deeply silent. Except for the driveway pebbles spelling out his name at the security gate, Prince had managed to erase nearly all traces of his existence in this landscape.

The wind stirred the tall grasses that shot up through the snow, quiet and wild at once. In 1981, when Prince was twenty-two, he told a reporter he'd changed his address in Minneapolis thirty-two times. "There was a great deal of loneliness," Prince said. There is probably a straightforward explanation for why Prince destroyed so many of the houses he lived in—tax reasons or privacy—but I had begun to think of it in ritualistic, agricultural terms, an artist adopting the slash-and-burn farming method to encourage regrowth, forward movement. The month before he died, Prince had announced his forthcoming memoir. Elsewhere in Minneapolis he had started researching his own houses too. And making pictures.

Alda Le Shay Reed lives on Logan Avenue in north Minneapolis with her father and her sons Jayon, who just turned ten, and Zyier, who just turned five, the age Prince was when he last lived at this site. Alda is twenty-eight; she works in health insurance, but she might like to be a makeup artist one day, or even a singer. This childhood home of Prince's was destroyed, too—the house that stands there now, owned by Alda's mother, was built in its place. "I always predicted he would come back here," said Alda Burnaugh-Johnson, who moved away not long before this came true.

"So it was late July 2015, just a year before he died," Alda Reed began. "Nine months," her mother interjected. The walls behind them were painted a goldish shade; a mosaic of mirror shards, installed by the elder Alda, framed another mirror. Prince would have admired this, I thought.

"And it was a Saturday," the younger Alda continued, "and it was early in the day and it was crazy 'cause nobody was on the block but me, not even any cars out there but mine. It was hot out and I was on the phone, and I said to my friend, hold on, I think somebody is out here taking pictures. And I go up to this person, like, 'Why you taking—,' and then I'm like, 'You're Prince! *You're Prince!*' And he just looks at me and kind of smiles and bats his eyes, and he says, 'No, I'm not.' And I'm like, 'Yes, you *are* him!' I asked if he was here because he used to live here, and he said yeah. He said he was doing something on his life. He asked *me* if *I* had a business card."

"When she called me," Alda's mother said, "she told me, 'Mama, I should've picked him up and held him till you got here so you could see him.'"

"To tell you the truth, my hands were shaking so bad I couldn't even ask him for a picture; I pretty much ran away from him," Alda said. "He had an Afro and a beanie on over it and a long sweater like what I have on, and he had on shades. They had parked at the corner, him and the woman who was actually taking the pictures. They were driving a little black Corvette. Everybody thinks it must've been red, but it was black."

Just out of her sight, Zyier silently scaled a kitchen counter, in search of a promised cupcake. Another kitchen cabinet was filled with microphones. "Me and my dad, we all do karaoke all the time," Alda said. "Zy, now, he's very quiet, he's very reserved. The teachers thought he didn't know how to talk. He just didn't want to talk to *them*. When kids speak to him, he acts all shy; he just smiles and keeps on walking. But I think he'll be a singer one day. He loves to sing. When my dad starts playing old songs, he sings along."

From around 1965 to 1970, Prince lived at 2620 8th Avenue, less than a mile away from Alda's house. It was while living here, at age ten, that he saw James Brown perform and got to dance onstage with him. During his time here he is said to have written his first song, "Funk Machine," on his father's piano. The house is painted yellow. When we returned one late afternoon, a single outdoor bulb glowed bright yellow. The mailbox bulged with envelopes that looked as if they'd been rained on and dried out again; in every window the shades were drawn.

In a side yard, dried flowers rose up, straw-like survivors of the winter, a hazy gold. I wondered if this house was always this color, and if that is what had drawn Prince to the yellow house in Chanhassen. I wondered if he and his photographer had come back to make a picture of this place too. I supposed it didn't matter, after all, that no one was home.

Originally published on Vogue online on April 21, 2018.

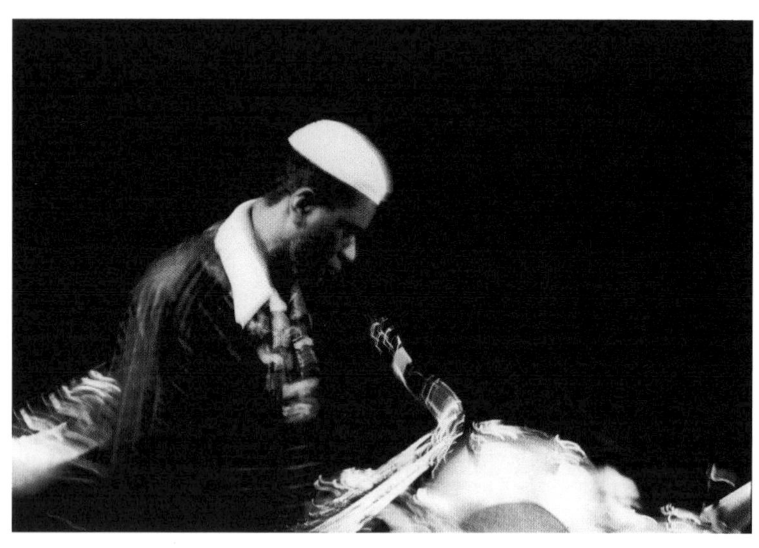

Ming Smith, *Pharoah Sanders at the Bottom Line*, New York, 1977

Trail Blaze in an Electrifying Blur: Ming Smith and Her Muses

Ming Smith very nearly turned down the Museum of Modern Art. In 1979, the Ohio-raised artist and recent Howard University graduate had been living in New York City for only a few years, modeling for beauty advertising to pay the bills. When she dropped off her photography portfolio for review, a receptionist assumed she was a messenger, but when she returned to pick it up she was ushered immediately into the curators' offices. John Szarkowski, the museum's director of photography, wasn't in, but as curator Susan Kismaric explained, the museum was keenly interested in acquiring some of Smith's works. A price was named; Smith, who was used to putting her modeling earnings toward darkroom supplies, was taken aback. "That wouldn't even have paid for my expenses!" she told me of the figure. It is incredible now to think of any young artist telling MoMA no thanks, but Smith, whose extraordinary, humanist depictions are experiencing a quiet but welcome resurgence of attention, certainly did. Kismaric urged her to reconsider. Think about it over the weekend, she said.

Smith did reconsider, and that year she became the first Black woman photographer to have prints acquired by the museum's permanent collection. Today MoMA owns seven of her black-and-white works, including clear-eyed, graceful documentary photographs of mothers and children in Harlem. Also within the museum's holdings are flashes of the hand-colored and dreamlike multiple-exposure prints and electrifying blur Gordon Parks referred to when he wrote of her pictures years later in an essay for her 1991 monograph *A Ming Breakfast: Grits and Scrambled Moments*: "Wondrous stuff crops up in her imagery, stuffing itself into her sight."

"I always believed my work was bigger than me," Smith tells me. "And the MoMA was a milestone. But then for forty years there was nothing, no shows, no artist talks." When she says this, she's exaggerating a little, though not by much. The current revival of interest in her photographs was largely helped along by MoMA's *Pictures by Women: A History of Modern Photography*, a 2010 exhibition which recontextualized Smith's work alongside that of fellow experimenters in the form, including Diane Arbus, an influence, and Ming's friend Lisette Model. Writing in the *New York Times* of a solo show that same year at June Kelly Gallery, Holland Cotter praised Smith's "heartfelt and gorgeous" pictures: "It's hard to think of another photographer who could set a misty head shot of the writer James Baldwin in a bank of dark clouds over the Harlem skyline and get away with it ..." Last year, Steven Kasher Gallery hosted the first major retrospective of Smith's work; and after the 2017 Brooklyn Museum exhibition *We Wanted a Revolution: Black Radical Women, 1965–85*, "I had women telling me they cried when they saw my pictures," Smith says. This fall, as the Tate Modern–curated exhibition *Soul of a Nation: Art in the Age of Black Power* lands at the Brooklyn Museum, her pictures again gain a prominent place, perhaps pointing curators to bodies of work still largely unseen.

We are sitting in Smith's apartment, with its twin views: a window onto central Harlem where she lives now, and the living room, filled with evidence of the last four decades, piles of large framed prints, and massive, taped-up ones. The floors are heaped with more prints, framed and unframed, and boxes of slides. Smith darts around the room barefoot between them, with dancer-like elegance. Visible here are years spent in music and traveling the world, as during her marriage to jazz saxophonist

　　　　　TRAIL BLAZE IN AN ELECTRIFYING BLUR

David Murray (whose portrait is among the MoMA holdings). Smith's musician son Mingus, whom she had with Murray, sits at a small desk nearby, poring through his mother's digital archives as she pulls from distinct bodies of work, including an early 1990s series made in Pittsburgh in which Smith photographed people and places of the Hill District, the neighborhood where Pulitzer Prize–winning playwright August Wilson set *Fences*, *The Piano Lesson*, and other dramas in his Century Cycle. Smith's photographs walk back to Wilson's original artistic inspiration; as he once said of the paintings of Romare Bearden, a mutual influence: "What I saw was black life presented on its own terms, on a grand and epic scale, with all its richness and fullness, in a language that was vibrant and which, made attendant to every-day life, ennobled it, affirmed its value, and exalted its presence."

The presence of the "wondrous stuff" Parks wrote of is pal-pable in this room—the record of an artistic and adventurous sensibility that casts uncommon light on artists and little-known persons alike. The glitter and sequined cape of Sun Ra in Smith's famous portrait of the avant-jazz musician unfurls winglike over his shoulder, seeming to shed layers of stars in his wake, a cosmic path. Face up on another stack of prints is a portrait of Grace Jones, head ecstatically thrown back, in a wash of glitter that Smith enhanced with daubs of pink paint. Jones, who was starting out as a model at the same time as Smith, was a friend. "She called me and told me to come out to Studio 54 and take that one," Smith says. "I knew her before she was 'Grace Jones.' But then again, she already was. Grace was always so free."

Smith frequently refers to the most spectral moments in her work as "gifts," and light as "spiritual." Not religious, she clarifies—she means the way Rembrandt used light or the way Brassaï did. Sometimes the spirit manifests in multiple exposures that create stunning and surprising connections; sometimes it's simply the mystic, ghostlike blur in her portraits that suggests not just an instant, but a trail left behind. Smith's affection for her subjects is as evident in her portrait of Alvin Ailey as it is of mourners watching the great choreographer's funeral procession.

In 2001, after a dozen years living in Los Angeles, Smith returned to New York, the city that made her a photographer. She recalls her first move to the city, living in Greenwich Village, heading out on modeling go-sees and eating at cheap diners near Washington Square Park, where she sometimes ran into Lisette Model and her husband eating dinner too. Model's fearless street photographs were an early influence; she became a friend. "I would ask her questions about love!" Smith says.

Prior to her first acquisition by MoMA, Smith was invited by Lou Draper to join the African American photography collective Kamoinge, whose members included Roy DeCarava and Gordon Parks. She recalls meetings at Draper's studio around East 18th Street and Fifth Avenue "where all the photographers had studios then — Avedon, James Moore, Arthur Elgort," Smith says. "Lou Draper was a great, generous teacher. You felt safe with him." For her first forays into the darkroom, Smith had forgotten to buy a lens holder and Draper improvised one for her. "So that's where that started," Smith says of the handmade borders that still frame many of her prints with an imprecise, elegiac quality.

One of the core Kamoinge principles was the importance of Black photographers portraying Black people, which Smith seized with an instinctively surrealistic approach. When she photographed her writer and artist heroes James Baldwin, Romare Bearden, and James Van Der Zee, she says, "I needed to present them as they appeared to me: larger than life." The day I visit Smith happens also to be Baldwin's birthday, what would have been his ninety-fourth. Smith met him not in Harlem, the neighborhood of his birth and formative years, but France, where he spent most of the rest of his life. "I met him at a jazz festival there in the late 1970s," she says, "but here is where I really feel him. I wanted to show his presence in Black life in Harlem. I wanted to give you something else there, his spirit." It was a humid day in Harlem, and as I bid Smith and Mingus goodbye and walked out in the streets, violet-gray clouds grew and filled overhead,

     TRAIL BLAZE IN AN ELECTRIFYING BLUR

sending down a fine drizzle of rain and calling out the umbrella sellers who always seem to instantly appear out of nowhere on 125th Street at the first raindrop. Looking up at the sky, it was impossible not to think of Baldwin looming there. Smith, of course, had put the picture in my head.

Originally published on Cultured Mag online on September 18, 2018.

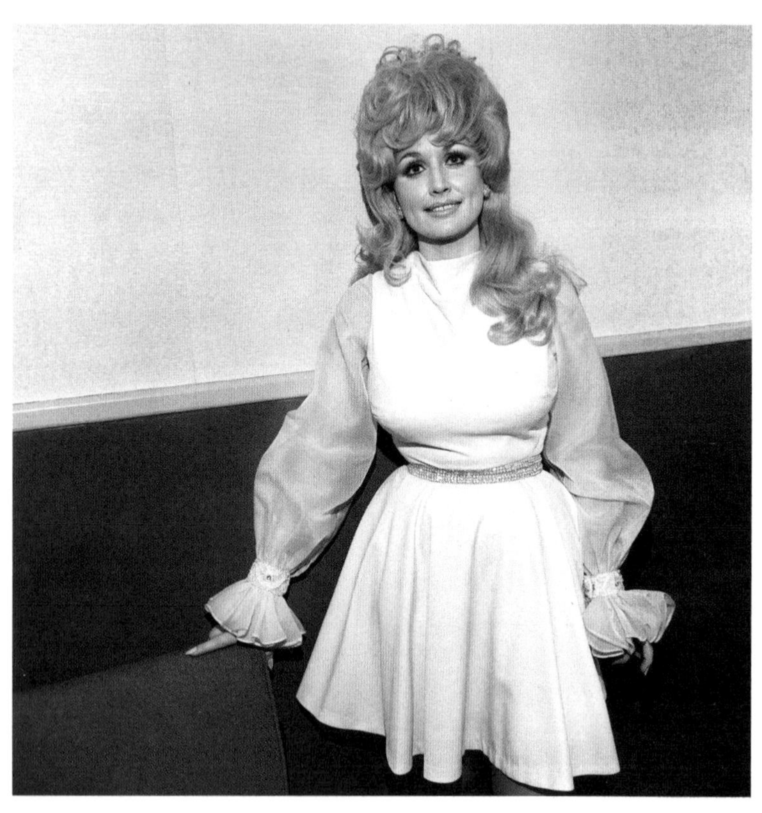

Henry Horenstein, *Dolly Parton, Symphony Hall, Boston, Massachusetts*, 1972

Close Up the Honky Tonks:
Henry Horenstein in 1970s Nashville

Last year on the Saturday after Christmas, I was driving a borrowed car alone at night through the Blue Ridge Mountains of Virginia into North Carolina with an iPod that suddenly refused to play. In silence I passed churches and discount stores and shuttered tourist roadside stands with a cartoonish mountaineer painted on billboards and decorative bales of hay scattered in their parking lots; a couple gas stations; a biker motel; a combination steak house and nightclub whose name, Top Cats III, alluded to the mystery of predecessors I and II. And then, for long stretches and deep curves, there was nothing. The roads were dark and winding, the radio waves vast and empty. I turned on the high beams and cruised through various static frequencies and switched, as one does in the less inhabited parts of the world, to AM, and there on WSM 650 I struck gold. Though the patch of black highway I was traveling felt like the dead of the night, it was Opry time.

The Grand Ole Opry's first radio broadcast was ninety years ago this Saturday, and ever since, it and its sister programs have broadcast on a regular basis, these days at least twice a week. Though it's the longest-running radio program in the country, for decades claiming more listeners than any other show in the world, I can't claim to have regularly been among them. Precisely because I grew up in the same part of the country as the Opry meant I purposefully tried to get as far away as I could from its traditional country and bluegrass and mountain songs. But it also meant that country music would eventually hold as lasting an influence and remain as much of a fixture for me as the landscape surrounding me on that dark drive.

The Opry is always something old, something new. That night's featured performers included a sweet family band of bluegrass players from eastern Tennessee whom I could envision sharing the stage with the Carter Family some fifty years prior, as well as a newcomer who sang an ode to his boat and his truck. When the hosts called out the show's sponsors for the evening, they made the Dollar General sound like a down-home mom and pop store. Still, there was something strangely soothing about the whole experience, both constant and familiar, particularly as it segued practically seamlessly into the next show, also country, which honored call-in requests for songs by Opry legends Marty Robbins, the Louvin Brothers, Patsy Cline, Kitty Wells, and Little Jimmy Dickens. Over the decades, the Grand Ole Opry stars have been legion: Roy Acuff; Hank Williams, who after failing to appear at several shows was shorn of his membership just before his untimely death; DeFord Bailey, a harmonica player who holds the distinction of being the first musician announced as being of the Opry, back in 1926, as well as the show's first African American performer. More than forty years passed before Charley Pride became the second Black performer to be inducted, in 1993.

George Jones drove nearly eight hundred miles in a straight shot the night he was invited to debut on its stage and barely remembered a thing afterward. "A country singer making it to the Opry in 1956 was like an athlete making it to the Olympics," he wrote in his autobiography, *I Lived to Tell It All.* "I was simply too overjoyed to realize what I was doing." A young Johnny Cash tuned in from eastern Arkansas to listen to Ernest Tubb and Bill Monroe, and Willie Nelson tuned in from Texas to listen to Johnny Cash.

And before that, before he went outlaw country, let his hair grow and left Music City behind, Nelson had arrived in Nashville

　　　　　　　　　　CLOSE UP THE HONKY TONKS

as just another struggling songwriter, alongside Kris Kristofferson, Roger Miller, Harlan Howard, Hank Cochran, and Tom T. Hall, writing lyrics and playing music down at nearby Tootsies Orchid Lounge. "Nashville is a place where people get off the bus like Hollywood was many years ago," Robert Altman said of his 1975 film named for the Opry's hometown.

Those were some of the people photographer and film-maker Henry Horenstein was interested in when he set out on road trips from Massachusetts to Nashville in the early '70s. He wanted to take pictures of the fans, not the stars, but with right-place-right-time luck, he landed in town in the midst of one of the Opry's many golden eras, just before it left its longtime home at the Ryman Auditorium, referred to by Jones and Porter Wagoner and others as the Mother Church of Country Music. "It was a historic time, and I just happened to be there," says Horenstein, now a professor at the Rhode Island School of Design, who has also extensively photographed country music in Austin, Texas, and Bakersfield, California. He was around when the Opry celebrated its fiftieth anniversary, and more important, he went into the homes of musicians and to Tootsies and other bars in Nashville and beyond that served as the Opry's training leagues.

Photography figured into some of the lyrics of the songs written and sung in those places: "Pictures of Life's Other Side" (Hank Williams). "Old Photographs" (Charley Pride). "A Picture of Me Without You" and "Developing My Pictures"—both by George Jones, the latter with a deadpan line best sung in Jones's pliable, plaintive lonesome highway yearn: "My mind's my darkroom." The '70s represented a transition between Countrypolitan and the Nashville Sound to the Urban Cowboy era, writes legendary Opry announcer Eddie Stubbs in the introduction to Horenstein's photobook *Honky Tonk: Portraits of Country Music* (2003), which focuses on country bars from Nashville to New Hampshire: "[T]he honky tonk is a piece of Americana that is fading quickly into obscurity . . ."

Horenstein's newest book, *Histories: Tales from the '70s,*

features photographs of lesser-known people and places that formed the decade. On the eve of the Opry's nintieth anniversary, I spoke to him about the stories behind some of his photographs from *Honky Tonk*.

Rebecca Bengal: One of the first albums you ever bought was *Johnny Cash Sings Hank Williams*. What struck you about country music, growing up in New Bedford, Massachusetts?

Henry Horenstein: Basically, I like a good story, and country music in those days—not today—was folk music. You know, a lot of people called Hank Williams a folksinger during his time. Hank Williams was unusual in that he wrote a lot of his old songs. Johnny Cash wrote a lot of his first songs too. You can't call them troubadours exactly, but they had that kind of quality. The times people lived in—families and dying and wars and battles and just life—it made for this very rural music. One of my favorite country singers is Little Jimmy Dickens, who I got to photograph a couple times. He lived on a farm with twelve kids and slept in a little piece of the bed and got the north and south side of a chicken, is the way he put it—if he was lucky, you know, when the preacher came to dinner. So it's those stories that interest me.

RB: In your book, you make the point that back then, country music was everywhere.

HH: When I was a kid, it was all AM radio, there was no FM segmentation. Elvis had become a star, and they were looking for other Elvises. I mean, Elvis was a white country singer with a little bit of soul basically. They picked up all these guys who were handsome, nice-singing country singers and put them on the radio: Conway Twitty, Johnny Horton, Jerry Lee Lewis. Some of them had one or two hits and disappeared, but some of them had real careers.

By the time I got to high school it was the folk music days.

Paul Clayton, who helped me buy my first record, was a folksinger. Some of his records are on Smithsonian Folkways today, and he actually used to come and hang out in New Bedford when he wasn't in Greenwich Village. He was supposedly one of the models for the Coen brothers' Llewyn Davis character. He lived in New Bedford and he sang about Frankie and Johnny and Pretty Boy Floyd, as did Woody Guthrie, so I got to know that music. I didn't distinguish it as country music. And of course Bob Dylan was heavily influenced by country and went on to record in Nashville.

RB: Eventually you found yourself backstage at the old Ryman Auditorium.

HH: It's funny, you go to the Opry now as a photographer and if you've got credentials, you've got a PR person or two attached to you and practically pointing your camera for you. I've only been back a few times in recent years and that's exactly what happened to me. I was there the week that Johnny Cash died, and Kris Kristofferson was onstage. It was very special, you know, Kris is not a regular member of the Opry, so I don't know if he was there because he was close to Johnny and it was a tribute, or if it was a coincidence. The PR people were on me, though, the entire time.

RB: Sounds like you weren't that far off from a lot of the musicians and songwriters who rolled into Nashville trying to make it back then.

HH: There's this picture I took of a harmonica player at Tootsies Lounge—the guy had just come in from Florida, he had a couple weeks off from his job. I think he was a trucker and he was hoping someone would discover him. Sometimes they knew enough to make demos and Tootsie would put them on the jukebox. Everyone thought that was real generous of her, but the thing was, the guy was sitting there feeding the jukebox for his song the whole day, so she was making bank on him!

My own concerns were pretty basic back then. You know: Can I get laid? Can I afford weed? Can I buy a camera? Can I get the picture? If I could do all of that, then it was good. If I didn't get some of that going, then it wasn't good. To be blunt, that's all I really cared about.

RB: You were working mostly intuitively. What were some of those backstage encounters like?

HH: The historian E. P. Thompson was my hero; he was all about the importance of preserving the culture and not about the big stars of the day. That was a lesson I took into photography. So I consciously was not looking to photograph celebrities. Fortunately, I happened to without meaning to. This is how naive I was; I didn't realize musicians might actually *want* me to photograph them. I thought I was imposing on them.

When I photographed Dolly Parton, it wasn't at the Opry, but I didn't realize that she understood that the more photographs she got out there, the better it was for her. So when I went into the Opry I was kind of shy, but finally I started asking a little bit if I could photograph. Then a couple musicians invited me into their homes, which blew my mind. One was Del Reeves—he passed away a couple years ago, he had that trucking song "Girl on the Billboard"; also, Wilma Lee and Stoney Cooper, who were wonderful old-time musicians from WWVA radio and were very sweet. I didn't realize none of these people were very wealthy. They weren't living extravagantly; they had very middle-class lives. I'm sure it was a big improvement over how they were living when they got to Nashville, but they didn't have a lot of means.

RB: When you photographed Dolly Parton, she wasn't massively famous yet.

HH: I loved her then, there was no question. I loved her music, I had her records, some of the early stuff she made before she went with RCA. I went with some of the people on Rounder Records, we were doing a shoot for a little weekly paper, the *Boston Phoenix*. I was thinking, "Oh, my God, she's beautiful," and I was intimidated. Many of the photographs in *Honky Tonk* happened very, very quickly, some of them just in an instant. With Dolly, though, I had about an hour with her because she was waiting backstage for Porter [Wagoner] to call her out to sing.

RB: You have great photographs in *Honky Tonk* of Tootsies Orchid Lounge and some of the other Nashville bars, places which I imagine as being full of a bunch of superstitious songwriters sitting around writing out lyrics on bar napkins. Is that a total fairy tale or is that how it was then?

HH: That is how it was, definitely. I think, of course, Nashville is a lot of things to a lot of people. But you don't go into those bars on Lower Broadway to work in anything but music. It's all about the music. You weren't going to move to Nashville to work in a shop or a bar unless you thought it would help your career along. A lot of people come close. There's a lot of deep potential in these stories.

Originally published on Vogue online on November 23, 2015.

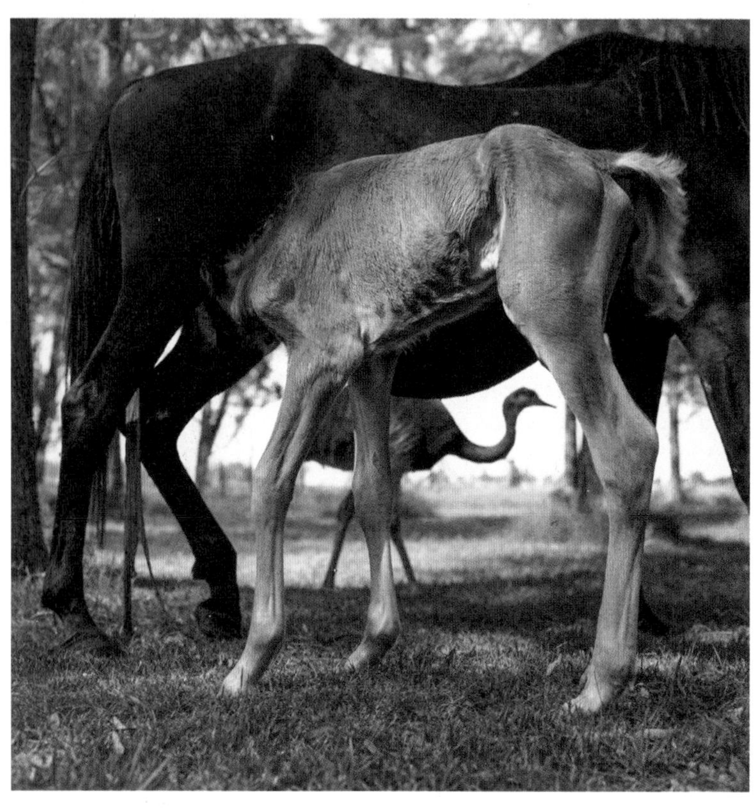

Alessandra Sanguinetti, *Milagros*, 1997

The Enormity of the Moment: Life and Death on an Argentinian Farm

A pack of dogs snarls at a pig. Chickens regard the lifeless fetus of a calf. A wild ostrich strolls nonchalantly by, visible underneath the body of a mare nursing its foal. Looking out over the bed of the pickup that delivered it here, a brand-new arrival, a duckling covered in yellow fuzz pops up out of a cardboard box, apprehensively regarding its new home, the approaching chickens and beasts, the sweep of life rushing over the dirt towards the truck.

Like creation stories, in which time collapses the entire arc of life, the sequence of photographs that make up Alessandra Sanguinetti's 2005 book *On the Sixth Day* seem to simultaneously inhabit a single day, and a lifetime. The title is borrowed from the Book of Genesis, pointing to the origin story of land animals, and the essential holiness of bearing witness to the lives and deaths of other creatures.

As a child growing up in Buenos Aires, Sanguinetti made an altar for her stuffed animals. "I mixed up my mother's perfumes and put them in a little airplane whiskey bottle and I would grab the animals and pray to an animal god I had made up," she said recently from her studio in California. On weekends and summers her family went to the *pampas*, the endless agricultural lowlands outside the city. When she was seven, her father bought a farm for raising cattle, situated near other, centuries-old farms where wild ostriches roamed alongside goats and sheep and horses.

"When the sheep were rounded up every week for food, I would know one of them would be killed, and I would viscerally feel like I was one of them," she says.

Sanguinetti was in her twenties when she enrolled at the International Center of Photography. These childhood images of animals began returning to her as ideas for pictures, in a much-mythologized and respected territory—the *campo*, the country. "It's such a part of Argentinian identity," she says. The photos that existed of the place failed to match what it meant to her. Photographers tended to render the flat horizon of the *pampas* in a melancholic black and white, pictures emphasizing qualities of "emptiness and desolation," Sanguinetti said. "On the other side of that was the cliché of the sunset and the gaucho galloping through the water."

Such images deadened and paled next to her own memories. "I'd think of the countryside—blue, green, red, brown," she said. "That's all the colors there are in the *pampas*, really: the blood, the sky, the grass, and the dirt." In the pictures she would later make, the palette of primary colors and earth is rich, ravishing, and even a bit lurid and fantastical, echoing Hans Christian Andersen, the Brothers Grimm, the story of The Devil with the Three Golden Hairs. "I unfolded it in a fable-like manner, emulating the stories I grew up on in order to make the familiar and ordinary, extraordinary."

The attendant vision, the painterly composition, and embrace of contrasts in the work of Joel Sternfeld and the enmeshed perspective of Nan Goldin, both early influences for Sanguinetti, can be thought of as unconscious guides to these photographs. Embedded in them is a watchfulness open to the miniature, divergent narratives unfolding in the center and at the edges of the frame, some occurring so quickly that they threaten to be swallowed up and forgotten in the swirl and cycle of daily life. "A chick escaping over the fence, or a mother separated from her calf," Sanguinetti said. "All these dramatic things were happening and no one seemed to acknowledge the enormity of the moment."

What appears through the sequencing of the book to occur in a single, monumental day is the product of photographs Sanguinetti made over time between 1996 and 2004, when she was working as a photo editor at a newspaper with a generous supply of film and a supportive boss. Almost every Friday, she'd raid the film refrigerator and take her Hasselblad into the country, most often to a neighboring farm, where she fell back into the rhythm of childhood. "One of my favorite things to do is just sit in a field," she said, "and wait for the cows to notice me and come over. They're very curious. I would take pictures of them while lying down on the grass. I just started getting on my knees instinctively."

Like Barbara Gowdy's 1999 novel *The White Bone*, a radically moving, fully realized epic told entirely from the perspective of elephants in the wild, Sanguinetti depicts the emotional lives of the animals who regard the deaths of their fallen comrades with seeming empathy, or sometimes coldness, or sometimes with apparent recognition of their own mortality. Whether or not any of this is possible or real is beside the point. Her photographs entreat the human viewer to participate simply as a fellow animal.

This is partly achieved through a deliberate resizing. Like William Eggleston's famous 1969 photograph of a tricycle, viewed so that it seems the same size as the sedan parked in the background, her animals are scaled in equal importance to the humans in their midst. A duck noses at the worn feet of the farmer, Juana, whose leg bears a bloody gash from some working accident, whose canvas slippers sink into the mud. "I only included people when it had to with the animals' point of view," she says. "I wasn't trying to show people's complexity or a human point of view. I saw them as other creatures interacting with animals."

Sanguinetti was struck by Isaac Bashevis Singer's 1962 novel, *The Slave*, whose titular character Jacob is a cowherd in a seventeenth-century mountain village in Poland where he falls in love with his enslaver's daughter. A devout vegetarian, Jacob contemplates his relationship with the animals he is charged with tending. "He silently blamed the Creator for forcing one creature to annihilate another. Of all the questions he asked about the universe he found this the most difficult," Singer wrote.

Sanguinetti started spending long days and hours at Juana's farm, following her around as she worked. "I began to see how she embodied the dualism in our relationship to animals," she said. On occasion Sanguinetti felt guilty if an animal was killed and she *didn't* take a photograph. "Taking a photograph has always been about paying attention, and that inherently involves some kind of respect because you are taking the time to understand it. I can't photograph something I really don't love or am not curious about or don't respect in some way."

Meanwhile another, human story would intrude, in the form of Juana's nine-year-old granddaughters, cousins Guillermina and Belinda, who were the youngest persons on the farm and therefore unencumbered by duties, instead being free to play and dream as Sanguinetti once had. Her attention drifted away from the reality of the farm and into the imaginative world of the girls, marking the formative days of what would become her next project, one that continues even as the girls are no longer girls but women and mothers: *The Adventures of Guille and Belinda and the Enigmatic Meaning of Their Dreams*.

But the creatures of *On the Sixth Day* never left her. Three autumns ago, when Sanguinetti and I met in North Dakota to collaborate on a story on the Standing Rock Sioux–led resistance against the Dakota Access Pipeline, we spent the first day following a horse ride meant to commemorate the planned route of the pipeline. The night before, one of the animals had been badly injured— a teenage water protector had taken it out on a night ride without permission and it had gotten hurt. I watched Sanguinetti approach the horse, sequestered in a makeshift corral for rehabilitation. She moved gently around the animal and the hay spread out on the ground at its feet, listening, looking intently. When the horse lay down briefly in pain, she dropped to the grass too.

Originally published on Magnum Photos online on September 27, 2019.

 THE ENORMITY OF THE MOMENT

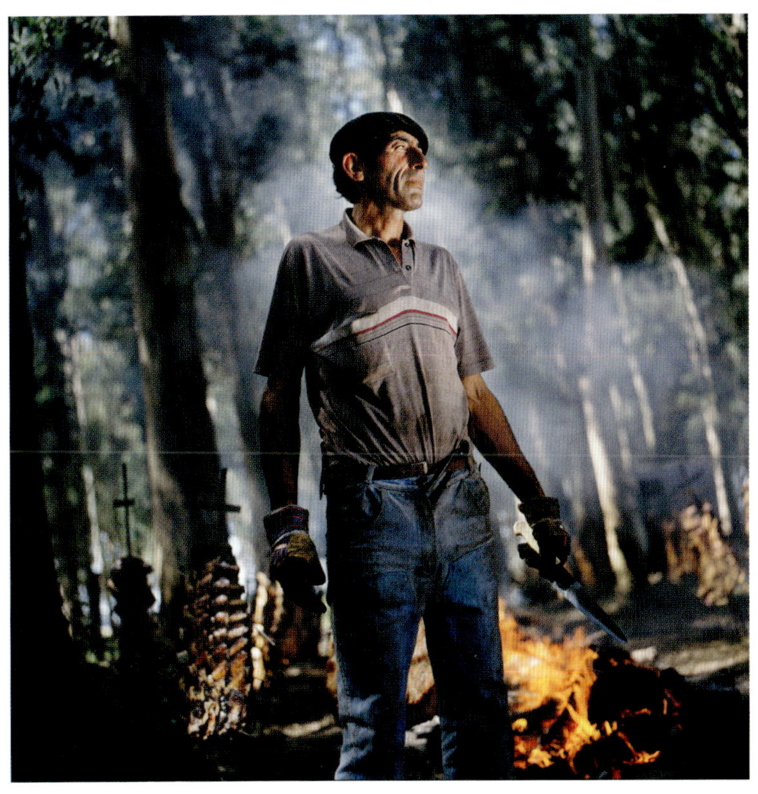

Alessandra Sanguinetti, *El asador*, 1996

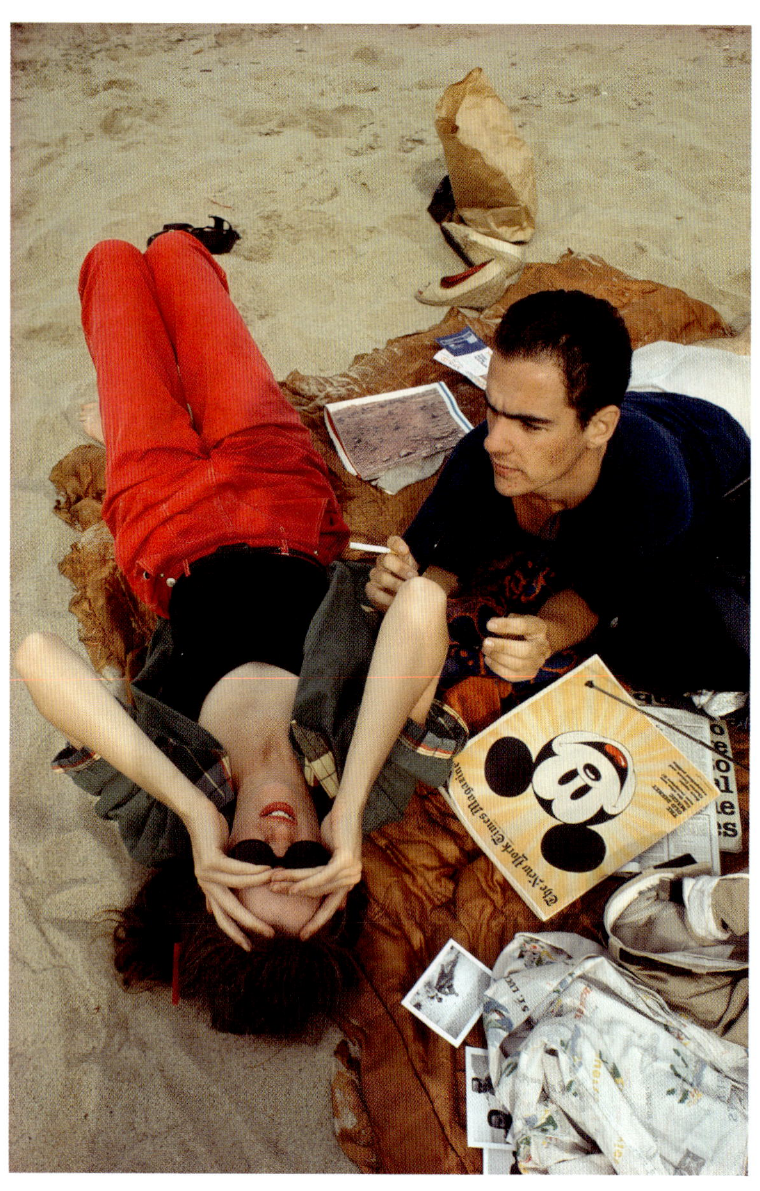

Nan Goldin, *C.Z. and Max on the Beach, Truro, Mass.*, 1976

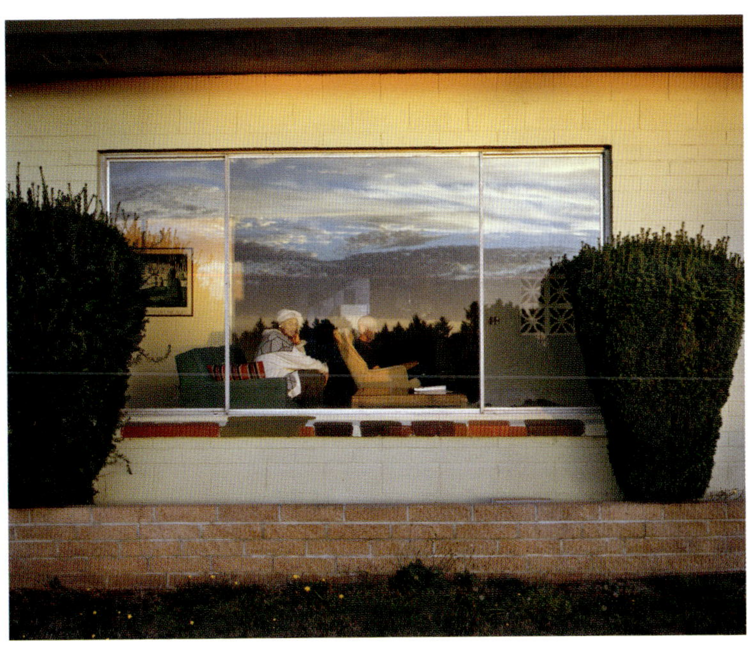

Curran Hatleberg, *Lost Coast (26)*, 2014

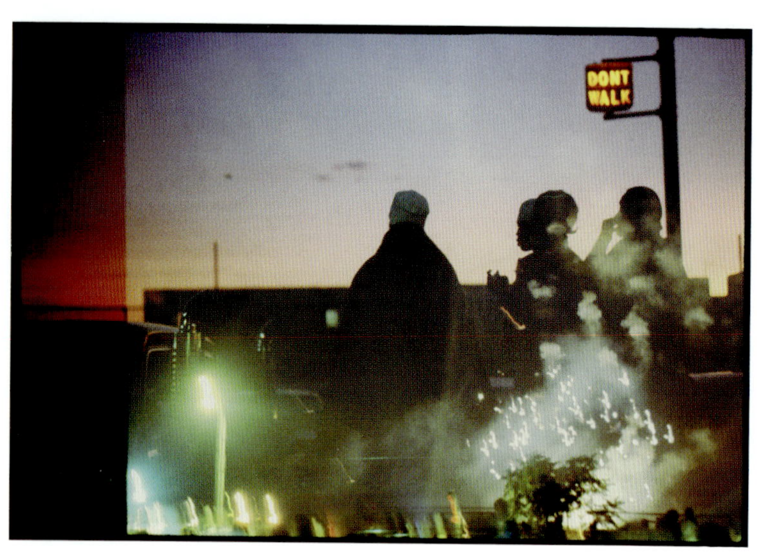

Ming Smith, *Acid Rain ("Mercy Mercy Me," Marvin Gaye)*, ca. 1977

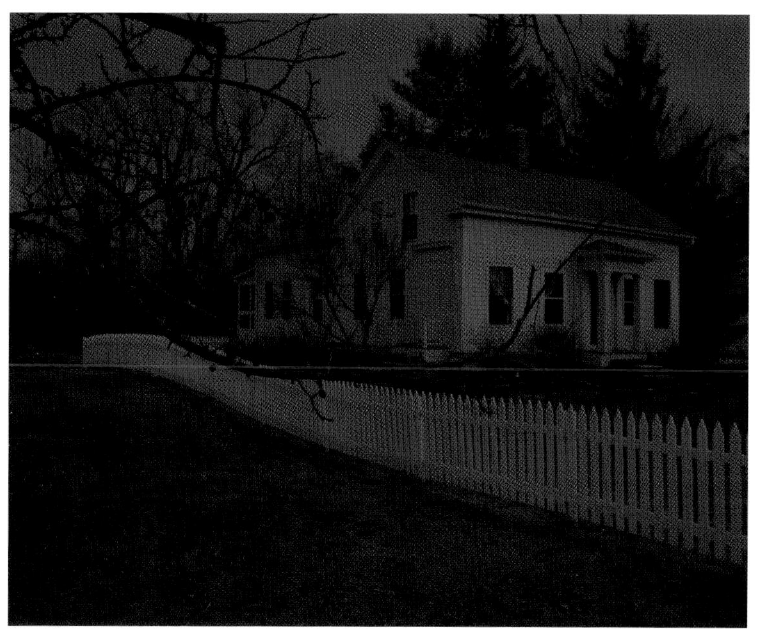

Dawoud Bey, *Untitled #20 (Farmhouse and Picket Fence I)*, 2017

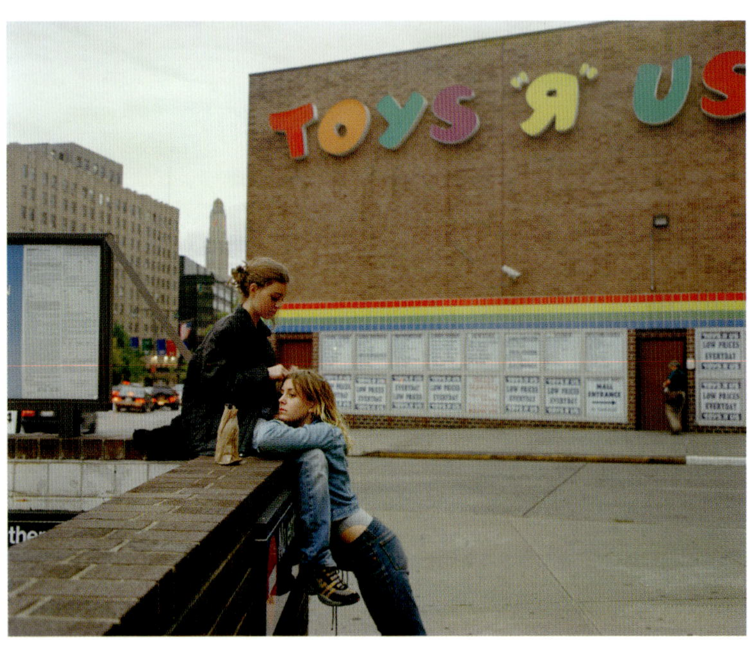

Justine Kurland, *Toys R Us*, 1998

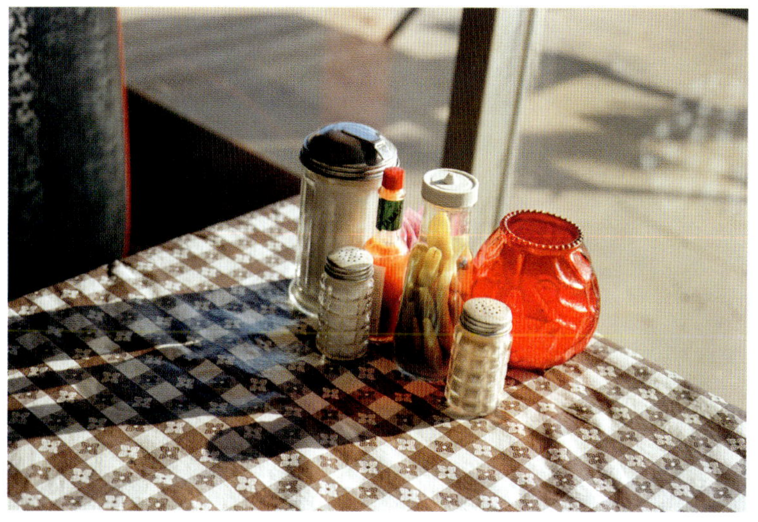

William Eggleston, *Untitled*, ca. 1983–86

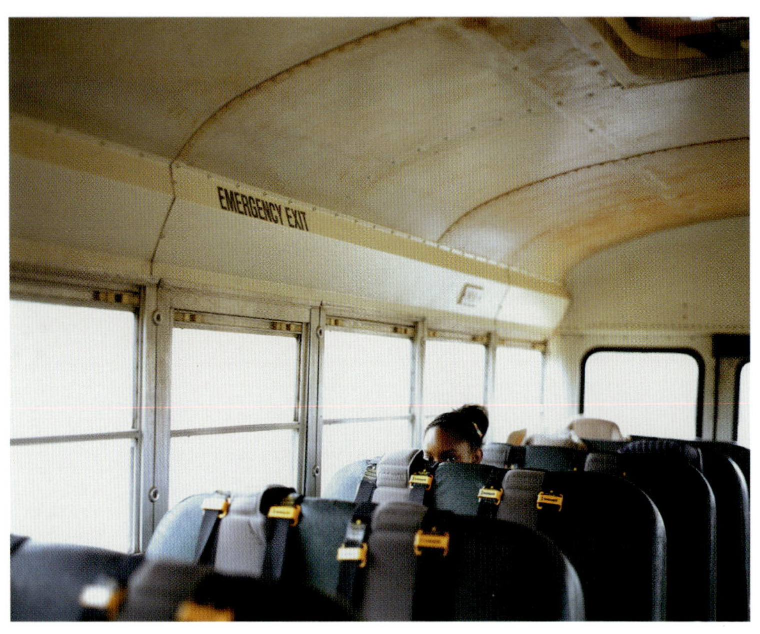

RaMell Ross, *Here*, 2012, from the series *South County, AL (a Hale County)*, 2012–14

And the Clock Waits
So Patiently

Time, unfortunately, though it makes animals and vegetables bloom and fade with amazing punctuality, has no such simple effect upon the mind of man. The mind of man, moreover, works with equal strangeness upon the body of time. An hour, once it lodges in the queer element of the human spirit, may be stretched to fifty or a hundred times its clock length; on the other hand, an hour may be accurately represented on the timepiece of the mind by one second.

—Virginia Woolf, *Orlando: A Biography*

I don't know whose side you're on,
But I am here for the people
Who work in grocery stores that glow in the morning
And close down for deep cleaning at night

—Jericho Brown, "Say Thank You Say I'm Sorry"

NOW, WHEREVER AND WHENEVER THAT IS FOR YOU

Dark stars inked on the palm of a raised hand. A tiny black-bird alone in the gaping, giant world of a street curb. Someone crouching in asphalt-baked sun in a position of prayer or pain or ecstasy, or perhaps all of the above. A guy kneeling to cut open a watermelon as two mothers perch on the edge of a gas station parking lot, their kids swarming close. The craggy shadow in the desert cast by a rock face; the man in a poncho crossing a thin creek over tall, shadowy grasses. The herculean act of pushing a massive tree down the middle of a rural street. A young boy fitting his small body in the space between tire rim and hub of a car, draped around the curve of the wheel. The frozen, shouting faces of a lineup of white cheerleaders some sixty years ago and, in an image from perhaps the same year, a white mother teaching her little girl to shoot a gun. A deer running down a highway embankment, between roads.

We know that a photograph lives in multiple eras at once: the time of its making, the time of its unveiling, the time of its subsequent rediscovery. Lazy language has us reaching for the trope of "capturing" "a moment." Similarly it is ingrained in us to look at photographs as stilled time, as past. But even this is a relative condition. The perception of the past is split in the act of remembering: how a moment first appeared, how it is seen differently later and reseen again, taken out of isolation, reshaped by knowledge and context. How the singular is part of a larger sequence.

When the experience of the present is overwhelmingly and radically altered, the grammar of time is disrupted too. Verbs no longer conjugate cleanly into their compartmentalized dimensions of past, present, and future; actions and thoughts loop back on one another. Linearity disappears. An analog clock, repetitive and circular, winding and ticking, is more relevant than the calendar. Strike twelve once again. Sometimes we inhabit all the tenses and eras at once.

As I lived with the images in *But Still, It Turns* over many months, as they became markedly more immediate, speaking with startling prescience to unfolding events that they preceded by years, that they had perhaps on some level intuited, I began to understand

     AND THE CLOCK WAITS SO PATIENTLY

their shared subject as the nature of time itself: how we perceive it, how we exist in it, how it exists in us, how it connects us.

PAST TENSE

On a cold, bright day at the end of January 2020, I sat with Paul Graham in Manhattan, photobooks spread over a tabletop, looking through the images he was considering for the exhibition *But Still, It Turns* (2021) by photographers and filmmakers whose work I had come to know within the past couple of years, some within the past several decades.* As the pages turned, as books opened and piled up and were rearranged next to each other, subtle connections began to reveal themselves like reshuffled cards. The luminous, anxious, and hardened men wandering harsh Western landscapes in Kristine Potter's Colorado (*Manifest*) and the Black young men outnumbered by a throng of white boys and men prowling a rocky riverbed in Stanley Wolukau-Wanambwa's *One Wall a Web*. The isolated beauty of Gregory Halpern's half-fictional Southern California (*ZZYZX*) brushing up against the clamor of individuals in the Northern California front yards, railroads, and parking lots through which Curran Hatleberg's camera seems to practically trespass upon (*Lost Coast*). The churches and lonesome kitchen tables and cluttered bedrooms (Richard Choi's unpublished project *What Remains*), which are so wholly interior that they could ostensibly belong to anywhere in the world. The brightly painted car washes and check-cashing storefronts contrasted with the empty, spackled-over walls where pictures once hung, contrasted with the people who used to live among those pictures (Piergiorgio Casotti and Emanuele Brutti's *Index G*). A teenage son and father on the sidewalk suited up in Sunday best, the young man tugging gently, endearingly, on his father's ear (Vanessa Winship's *she dances on Jackson*). The three youths, probably, though each has their black hoodies up, sitting in a swing set, facing a fence, the woods. Only the dog beside them meets the gaze of the camera (RaMell Ross's

South County, AL [a Hale County]).

As we talked, I began to imagine how the images would recalibrate once they were hung together on museum walls, shuffled again, how they would inevitably take on new meaning when seen in another time and place: fall 2020, just ahead of the US presidential election. While it is accurate to say that, with these bodies of work, Wolukau-Wanambwa, Winship, Ross, Potter, Curran Hatleberg, Halpern, Choi, and the collaborative team of Casotti and Brutti are each operating somewhere within the geographic landscape and psychic terrain of the United States of America, such an assertion feels heavy-handed. These are works that resist that kind of statement-making definition. These are works that resist easy categorization, too, slipping somewhere in the boundaries between genres. Realism is only a starting point, a lure.

"My work begins with the 'notion' of documentary," Gregory Halpern has said of *ZZYZX*, his 2016 photobook, which takes its title from a village on the edge of the Mojave Desert, and which summons a California both real and imagined, downtrodden and mystic. The village is, alphabetically, the last named town in the California atlas, but figuratively it is a stand-in for a half-imagined setting of drenched light and Joshua trees and bus stops and boardwalk and open horizon. Documentary is an entryway to fiction. Similarly to when he began making his film *Hale County This Morning, This Evening*, a 2019 nominee for the Academy Award in Documentary, RaMell Ross deliberately invoked "documentary's language of truth." "You use the documentary genre because it's a space where people are predisposed to truth, which is a great, great entryway into an idea," Ross said. "The premise of truth puts viewers in the frame of mind to receive larger truths."

A quiet fell over the Metrograph theater in New York City after a screening in 2018, as if to extend the spell of what we had all just seen. One of the principal aims Ross outlined in his manifesto for the film, to "participate, not capture," calls to mind Roy DeCarava, who, working from the forties through to the nineties, subverted the traditions of social documentary photography.

His deliberately subjective pictures affirm instead the camera's capacity for what he described as "creative expression." As Teju Cole has written, DeCarava "insisted on finding a way into the inner life of his scenes."

PAST PRESENT

Cut, shuffle, deal again. Looking at the photographs in January, when we still thought the most ominous event in the near future pointed to November 3, 2020, I was also reminded of *Election Eve*, the body of work William Eggleston made in October 1976 when a magazine, which Eggleston has variously recalled as *Rolling Stone* and at other times as the *New York Times Magazine*, asked him to make a photo essay set in Plains, Georgia, hometown of the then-little-known Democratic presidential candidate Jimmy Carter. Eggleston started photographing before he left his own city, Memphis, avoiding the tropes of the campaign trail and heeding a path instead of lonesome street corners, trees swaying in stormy cotton fields, porches strewn with tobacco spit cans, tin roofs rusting on abandoned houses, churches with hand-painted names in crooked lettering, weeds poking through red Georgia clay. The most overt marker of time and place is a LET'S ELECT JIMMY CARTER PRESIDENT sticker plastered to the bumper of a Chrysler in a rain-puddled parking lot. In the stillness of these almost entirely unpeopled shots there emerges a profound sense of anticipation, the elegiac resilience of unseen roadsides, rural cemeteries, houses barely stirring on hot afternoons. Carter won the election, the magazine never published the pictures (though in 1977, Eggleston produced a limited-edition portfolio of one hundred prints, which was reissued as a book four decades later) and those overlooked settings and things went on simply being, in the last days before Plains would be seen differently, before the people of the town would perceive it and themselves differently. "Only children, and older residents in memory, will have unstrained access to Plains as it appears here," Lloyd Fonvielle wrote in a preface. Hovering on its edges, Eggleston simultaneously delivered a picture of his own way of working: alighting on these subtle but telling signs in the landscape, as they unconsciously guided his path, pieces of a larger whole.

Sign-following. The photographers and filmmakers featured in *But Still, It Turns* are connected through a way of working that is similarly intuitive and unpremeditated, one that is not so much interested in the decisive moment as in the accumulation of them, or of the moment before, during, and after—building from one to the next.

It involves relinquishing control and yielding to chance encounters, trusting in the significant random reveal of the dealt hand while also seeking to turn over the facedown cards. It involves a kind of looking that exists outside the documentary tradition, and outside the "documentary style" of Walker Evans. It relies not on capturing but on a receiving of the world: to invoke the title of DeCarava's famous collaboration with Langston Hughes, an engagement with "the sweet flypaper of life," in which past, present, and future enter the same current.

PAST IMPERFECT

The sense of dropping into that current—the continuous past— is rendered in a particularly acute way by some of the featured photographers who are coming from outside the United States. Fear, prompted by the awareness of "heteronormative white violence" in America, tinged Stanley Wolukau-Wanambwa's 2012 move from the UK to Richmond, Virginia, where he began graduate school. This was seven years before Kehinde Wiley's resplendent anti-Confederate sculpture *Rumors of War* would be permanently installed blocks from Monument Avenue, the city's wide, tree-lined street populated with statues of Confederate icons. This was seven and a half years before those monuments

                                        AND THE CLOCK WAITS SO PATIENTLY

would begin to be painted with messages of protest and tributes to stolen Black lives and toppled. But in 2012, when he began photographing the series *Our Present Invention*, they infused the landscape, totems to a legacy of white supremacy. Wolukau-Wanambwa went off the path. Traveling on a bicycle made for a slowed, incremental discovery of the city and its inhabitants. Often his present-day photographs, whether of a newspaper opened to a story of Barack Obama celebrating the fiftieth anniversary of the passage of the Civil Rights Act, or a cutout figure of John Wayne, also contain the shadow of the photographer—the past viewed by the present, mingled within it.

Crossing the borders of a vastly divided American city, where the sense of the past lurking below the slick surfaces of the present is at the heart of Piergiorgio Casotti and Emanuele Brutti's *Index G* too. The Italian photographers embedded themselves in Saint Louis, Missouri, the sixth most segregated city in the United States. A conceptual framework—the Gini Index, a statistical measure of racial inequality—gave them permission to stray from it and also to render it in visual, real-life terms. The exterior pictures wander through the streets, landing on storefronts in benign palettes or saturated, commercial-friendly color, and peel back and forth, Oz to Kansas, Kansas to Oz, to mostly vacated interior rooms shown in black and white, evocative of past lives and memories. Portraits of the city's Black residents, also photographed in black and white, link the exteriors and these emptied spaces by simply transcending them. With subtle changes in expression, and minor shifts in pose, they are depicted across several frames, a choice that endows them with the semblance of motion and, thus, life. Viewed in contrast to the unpeopled street scenes and empty interiors, they are resonant—taken beyond the city's archaic borders, lifted briefly out of time.

Time is equally if differently slippery in the pictures of the UK-born artist Vanessa Winship. Apart from subtle details that date them—tattoos, for example—her American settings of riversides, rodeos, and beaches appear decadeless, an experience enhanced by Winship's dedication to black-and-white photography. Winship's arrival in the United States, after years of doing work in the countries of the Balkans and the Black Sea, ushered in what she has termed "a new period of receptivity" in an anxious personal time. The portraits of persons from those photographic encounters are like verbs activating Winship's long sentences of travels through silvery winter trees wispy with Spanish moss or filled with migrating birds. They filter through her pictures the way Kristine Potter watches her rugged drifters traverse the West, the way the shadow of Wolukau-Wanambwa's camera clouds his frames, the way RaMell Ross intersperses a 1913 clip of the brilliant performer and director Bert Williams, the first Black American actor to star in a feature film, so that Williams, a Black man performing in blackface, appears to encounter a plantation house in Hale County, Alabama, still standing a hundred and fifty years after the abolition of slavery, a century after his own time. The past and present fuse together as if in one extended day, one extended century, and coursing into our own.

AGAIN, THE PAST

Sign-following. Like Gregory Halpern, who chose the locations for *ZZYZX*, often utilizing Google Maps, Curran Hatleberg traveled around Humboldt County, California, to photograph *Lost Coast*. He operated almost purely by intuition to discover his settings, entering them unknown. "I can feel it come over me," he told the photographer Matthew Genitempo. "A place that's a sure thing will feel like a stage." Hatleberg possesses a Winogrand-like attention to the inner lives existing within large groups of people—a tableau of men sprawled on car hoods outside rodeos and shipyards; members of a family spilling out of a small house into the front yard, messy with life; and a handful of tiny distinct dramas playing out at once, a tangle of children and dolls and dogs and tossed-aside toys, a grill smoking. A sense of perpetual

     AND THE CLOCK WAITS SO PATIENTLY

motion courses through these photographs, as if the photographer drifted into them, as if they carried right on after the camera left.

This sense of the ongoing resonates with Paul Graham's work, which tends to linger over multiple frames, rendering the photograph as a moving, living thing. On that afternoon in January, we looked at the pictures some more. We spoke about this same feeling in them, the anticipation of life unspooling. *But Still, It Turns*. Later, I would realize, it had not occurred to me to ask about the origin of the title. It was a beautiful day and I walked off into cold bright sunlight. The world had not yet turned upside down.

ANCIENT PAST, SO TO SPEAK

In 1633, Galileo was forced to recant his heliocentric theory of the universe. "But still, it turns," he supposedly said after his meeting with the Roman Inquisition. Or, "And yet it moves." Or, "Albeit it does move." An account of Galileo's utterance of some form of the phrase first appeared in 1757. The moment he was set at liberty, the story goes, Galileo looked up to the sky and down to the ground and, stamping with his foot, in a contemplative mood, uttered, "*Eppur si muove*," that is, "Still it moves," meaning, of course, the Earth. The phrase "*E pur si muove*" [sic] appears in a painting of Galileo completed after his death. Whether he actually said it, or precisely what he said or not, is less interesting to me than why the Church stopped him. Why it insisted on the geocentric model. Why they were so threatened by a challenge to their understanding of the movement of the days.

It is February when I am having this thought. A million years ago.

TIME OUT OF TIME

"When someone has a terminal disease, the soothing churn of time is shattered," narrates the protagonist of Lucia Berlin's short story "Wait a Minute," at her sister's bedside. Time speeds frenetically; yet "turns sadistically slow." The horizon of death "rips up the calendar."

Inevitably, over the passage of time, pictures will hit differently. Mid-March, ten days into isolation, amid the abrupt reordering of a world in which human touch is now a transgression, in which the once close people in our lives become mere images, I am teaching creative writing classes from a converted motel room in Virginia not far from our shuttered classroom, from my sealed-off university office. Computer glow on my face, a darkening, ocean-fogged window behind me, we read fiction about mourning, a topic that months ago I had unwittingly placed on the syllabus for this date. Now, in March, *grief* was the word the world had chosen to collectively describe its swift unraveling.

Pandemic time is as twisted as grief time, as if operated by a sadistic roller coaster driver, moving with wrenching slowness and whiplash speed. It pulls out the days into endless stretches of locked-down sameness, while the incessant barrage of news adds so many new realities that twenty-four hours becomes seven days. A week ago you were someone else. A week ago was a decade and yet the morning would somehow never end. Last week we'd all vowed to write our *King Lear,* like Shakespeare in quarantine; this week we struggled to finish a paragraph. Now even completing a sentence was its own *Lear*, for adding that final punctuation signaled a moving on, a future. Three weeks in, the idea of the future veered from abstract to unfathomable.

There was solace in the promise of an exhibition perhaps still happening in the fall, or in the winter, as there is solace in the fact of the book containing these images. There was solace in the promise of future seasons, of 2021 arriving. It had been weeks since I'd spent time with these images. I was worried, I confess, that they'd fall short. In this cracked-open world would they seem archaic, irrelevant, things of the past?

          AND THE CLOCK WAITS SO PATIENTLY

March. But they couldn't have felt sharper, these portraits of loners and their places, most photographed several years ago, that seemed to spring straight from the present shutdown: Wolukau-Wanambwa's solo figures and crumbled facades and Hatleberg's young men loitering around the picnic tables outside a gas station, each lost in his own psychic zone; the wanderers in Potter's Colorado, in blasted white sunlight or in deep shadow, the way the long history of the land itself registers as hopeful resilience. From Casotti and Brutti, the image of a woman peering out through the thin strip of light in closed kitchen blinds, standing next to sparse and strange furnishings, a salon-style hair dryer making an alien shadow on the wall, a guitar amp, a teapot. The room is immaculate, the longing palpable. Another image, another room, Richard Choi: the sadness of suspenders and a TV tray. Pink tissue, a wall yellowed with lamplight. Another dimension opens up in Choi's accompanying video—there is solace in its perceived intimacy. The photograph is altered, reseen.

"Two different realities exist in the photo and the video," Choi later told me, referring to *What Remains*, a series that arose by chance too. When he began the MFA photography program at Yale, Choi was resistant to working in digital. Eventually he relented. While photographing with a new camera, he accidentally made a video. "It was as if the photograph had magically extended itself," he said.

Some of the people in *What Remains* are family members—his grandparents, his parents. Some are strangers Choi encountered at churches or passing by them on neighborhood streets. He photographs them inside their homes and up close, at 35mm, often focusing on the face, the hands. Accompanying each still photograph is a video, ranging in duration from a minute to an hour.

"I'm looking for these moments of solitude, so I just sit with them," Choi said. Sometimes there is stillness, or talk and, often, the vulnerability of prayer. "I try to keep the videos as easy as possible. I like the silence, or the music, that will sometimes break through." Ambient sound is crucial to these pieces, sometimes cuing the small shifts that guide each video, the small elements of surprise that inevitably occur in them and what follows. "I realized what I wanted was that before, during, and after," said Choi. "I wanted the photograph and the entire thing that occurred. I wanted all of it. I realized I was attuned to this idea of life unfolding."

FLASH BACK A HUNDRED YEARS

April. The culture is looking back a century ago, to another pandemic. What did we learn? How did artists and writers metabolize the collective panic and despair? The flu epidemic of 1918–1919 took fifty million lives, but its cultural impact was largely overshadowed by World War I. Its artistic trace surfaces in close portraits: the "jaundiced isolation" the critic Megan O'Grady describes in a self-portrait by Edvard Munch, made after he survived the flu. Munch was luckier than Gustav Klimt, painted on his deathbed in 1918 by Egon Schiele, who would also fall victim to the virus. Schiele's painting *The Family* from that year is an imagined portrait of himself, his wife, and the child they were expecting; a portrait that was never realized.

Yet the epidemic and the war alone did not precipitate a cultural movement as much as it did catalyze a sea change already underway. Literary Modernism has its precursors in Henri Bergson's theory of duration. Bergson's unscientific, subjective understanding of time is rendered most significantly in Virginia Woolf's *Orlando* and elsewhere: in *Mrs. Dalloway,* where the chiming of Big Ben is a perpetual reminder of the mingling of present action and memory, and in the section "Time Passes" from *To the Lighthouse*, a requiem of structureless grief.

                    AND THE CLOCK WAITS SO PATIENTLY

But what after all is one night? A short space, especially when the darkness dims so soon, and so soon a bird sings, a cock crows, or a faint green quickens, like a turning leaf, in the hollow of the wave. Night, however, succeeds to night. The winter holds a pack of them in store and deals them equally, evenly, with indefatigable fingers. They lengthen; they darken. Some of them hold aloft clear planets, plates of brightness.

— Virginia Woolf, *To the Lighthouse*

In the slippery, liquid, elastic time of 2020, we circle back to these shifts and forward again. When the order of the world is thrown into chaos, is objective experience, or a representation of it — a story, a photograph — even possible? When the world is called into utter suspicion, can time be considered absolute? And how then can films and photographs represent it? "Where does time reside?" RaMell Ross asks in *Hale County This Morning, This Evening.*

In 2009, Ross moved from Washington, DC, to Hale County, Alabama, where time, he wrote, existed in a "haptic lull." Ross had come to teach photography initially for two weeks, but felt an immediate love for the place and the people in it. Early on he met Daniel Collins and Quincy Bryant, who would become the two characters at the core of *Hale County This Morning, This Evening.* Three more years passed — Ross continued to teach; he coached basketball; he embedded himself into the lives of the people of Hale County, and was embraced by them. He remains committed to living and photographing there several months each year, working in large format and making films. When he began filming what would amount to 1,300 hours of footage, he wrote a manifesto for the film, a rigorous and blazing statement in its own right. With *Hale County This Morning, This Evening,* he set out to "exalt Black lives." The film would be structured around beauty, around "using time to figure out how we've come to see and be seen."

Hale County was photographed repeatedly during the twentieth century, resulting in a surfeit of images that have to be seen as a kind of truth—and creating an iconography that threatens to lodge the place and its people forever in the past. Hale County is home to the museum named for a safe house that sheltered Martin Luther King Jr. during a visit there, less than a month before he was assassinated. Some of the county's crumbling plantation houses continue to be rented out for destination weddings. Hale County was photographed by the documentarian Jack Delano, working for the Farm Security Administration in the Depression years. Its barns and fields and egg-carton crosses placed on graves and its Klan-haunted landscapes were photographed extensively by the artist William Christenberry, who died at eighty in 2016 and was born in Hale County months after James Agee and Walker Evans went to Hale County for the work that would become *Let Us Now Praise Famous Men*. In Agee's text and Evans's photographs, Black people were almost entirely absent. "Their faces were soft, secret, utterly without trust of me and utterly without understanding," Agee writes of meeting a young Black couple, a characterization that seems to reflect his own feelings, lodged in fear, guilt, and yearning. Long before and long after Agee and Evans, writes Scott L. Matthews in his book *Capturing the South*, both Black and white Hale County residents expressed resistance at being portrayed by outsiders, starting with a group of folklorists that came making pictures and collecting songs in the early 1900s.

Agee's descriptions of the passage of days in Alabama ("flying shadows," "satin rain") and the sensory qualities of Jean Toomer's 1923 *Cane*, a Modernist novel in vignettes rooted partly in the American South ("And the sweet earth flying from the thunder") reverberate in Ross's photographs and in his film's long tracking shots of cotton fields, the time-lapse footage of night-time clouds and stars, marking the days in a film that deliberately avoids a dramatic arc, or even scenes. "The struggle narrative really got to me—most of the stories about Blackness, because of the past, obviously, have a very specific poverty struggle, beginning and end, and that forecloses greater understanding of just general humanity," Ross has said. Freed of the pressure of a storyline, the film liberates itself from the historical narratives that surround Hale County and the South. It speaks to a sense of felt time lived in vastness, present and past and whole—"the middle and pure height and whole of summer and a summer night, the held breath, of a planet's year," as Agee wrote.

And yet time stops too. "Life changes in an instant. The ordinary instant," as Joan Didion wrote in *The Year of Magical Thinking*, her memoir that begins with the death of her husband John Gregory Dunne, a moment when everything changes and life also goes on. Another film would have pivoted its plot around the death that occurs in *Hale County This Morning, This Evening*, but here it arrives as it does in life, sudden and awful, not an end but a piece of the ongoing. The before, during, and after. Night, however, succeeds to night. Everything stops, but still it turns. Days and nights unspool in the endless rounds of a baby's playful laps around a room, but grief surfaces swiftly and without warning in a fast-food drive-through line, and grace comes flapping in the early gusts of an oncoming thunderstorm. A young boy spreads his arms wide, lets the wind whip through, and life unfolds again.

THE FUTURE PRESENT

"Which quarter of 2020 will you specialize in?" is a joke that has arisen lately among historians. Our awareness of time is anchored in the long-term past firmly fused into the now: the four-hundred-year-old legacy of slavery in this country, the even longer history of colonialism. Our awareness of time is tuned to the continuous twenty-four-hour present of protests enveloping deeply divided cities all over America, all over the world. Our awareness of time is rooted in the increment of 8:46—eight minutes and forty-six seconds, the initially reported amount of time that Minneapolis police officer Derek Chauvin pressed his knee into George Floyd's neck, the amount of time that none of his fellow officers stepped in to stop him, the amount of time it took for George Floyd's life to be stolen from him in a cruel and torturous end. Time turns sadistically slow.

On the cover of the June 22, 2020, issue of the *New Yorker*, the artist Kadir Nelson depicts the body of George Floyd standing tall and mighty and, within it, the bodies of Breonna Taylor, Rayshard Brooks, Ahmaud Arbery, Sandra Bland, Malcolm X, Medgar Evers, and Martin Luther King Jr. Floyd is a container for these and all the Black individuals violently killed in the United States by law enforcement and white supremacy before him. The images that define the present hold our past.

Stanley Wolukau-Wanambwa's *One Wall a Web* is a reassembling of history, a remade time, layered in contexts. Another way of looking: Wolukau-Wanambwa's work so aptly understands the dynamics at the root of our deepest rift that it is clairvoyant, predicting the pointed collage that played out on May 25, 2020. Early Memorial Day morning in New York, a white woman calling the police on a Black man bird-watching in Central Park invoked a casual and lethal form of racism deeply rooted in the American consciousness. That evening in Minneapolis, forty-six-year-old George Floyd violently forced to the pavement, pleading for his life and for his mother. Like the pairing of images and texts contained in a single book, the calendar emphasizes how Amy Cooper's call could have easily turned Christian Cooper's fate into George Floyd's murder. Just as a common last name is accidental, so is the shared date of these two unrelated incidents, both recorded on video. Coincidence intensifies the gravity of the first and makes evident its connectedness to the second: distant participants in the ongoing.

But how do we go on? How do we proceed? In an essay that marked the "abrupt shift" in his attitude toward the Velázquez painting *Las Meninas*, moving "from lingering exhilaration to vertiginous melancholy" during the early months of the pandemic, the critic Peter Schjeldahl imagined a future, months away, when we would be able to visit museums again, likely not in the flux of large crowds but in timed, spaced, set dimensions. What would being in those rooms feel like, in the after?

Everything in them will be other than what we remember. The objects won't have altered, but we will have, in some ratio of good and ill. The casualties of the coronavirus will accompany us spectrally. Until, inevitably, we begin to forget, for a while we will have been reminded of our oneness throughout the world and across time with all the living and the dead.

How will all these pictures read to you in the future unforeseen, months and miles away? Perhaps the pages of the book will make them more tangible, perhaps the pressing of the prints against each other will reshuffle the deck again, re-form their connections once more. They can't have predicted the world or know what will elapse in the time that stands between us now, how great the toll, at what grievous cost change may one day come. But still they saw the signs, and they shaped them. Now they join the long arc of time, they are its link. Picture them as the hands on the clock, slowing it down.

*Editor's note: The exhibition *But Still, It Turns: Recent Photography from the World* was presented at the International Center of Photography in New York, February 4–August 29, 2021.

Originally published in *But Still, It Turns*, ed. Paul Graham (MACK, 2020) and on the Paris Review online on February 11, 2021.

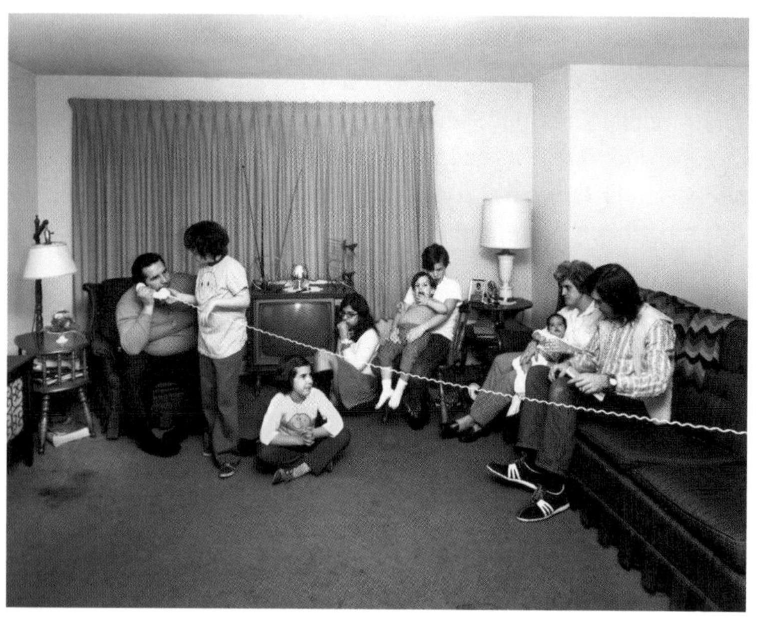

Chauncey Hare, *West Chester, Pennsylvania*, 1972

"This photograph was made by Chauncey Hare to protest and warn against the growing domination of working people by multinational corporations and their elite owners and managers."

Chauncey Hare's Protest

In the summer of 1979, as long lines queued up outside the San Francisco Museum of Modern Art for the highly anticipated arrival of *Mirrors and Windows: American Photography since 1960*, a John Szarkowski–curated exhibition, one man walked in the opposite direction. The show carried with it the electric buzz of a star curator redefining photography for a new age and anointing a current generation of photographers. Szarkowski divided them into two camps. There were the "mirrors," photographers he categorized as "romantic" and "expressionist," Robert Rauschenberg, Duane Michals, and Andy Warhol among them. Those in Szarkowski's "windows" group, whose work he called "realist" ("because no other word was better"), included Garry Winogrand, Diane Arbus, Lee Friedlander, Helen Levitt, William Eggleston, and Stephen Shore, as well as a rather intense-looking individual pressing fliers into the hands of passersby, demanding the removal of his own photograph and urging a boycott of the exhibition altogether. The flier called for outrage at the show's corporate sponsorship by tobacco giant Philip Morris.

On that day in June, Chauncey Hare was at the pinnacle of his photographic career. Two years earlier he had flown to New York for the opening of *The Effects of Technology on the Individual: Photographs by Chauncey Hare*, his solo show at the Museum of Modern Art, curated by Szarkowski. "I heard later that no one expected to see a short, knapsack-carrying, sandal wearing, ex-corporate engineer playing the role of a three-time Guggenheim Fellow photographer," Hare wrote of his Manhattan experience. He stayed at the West Side Y but was taken to lavish "expense account meals" (his characterization) with Aperture, who published his first book of photographs, *Interior America*, in 1978. Two months after Hare picketed *Mirrors and Windows*, Janet Malcolm reviewed *Interior America* alongside *Walker Evans: First and Last* (1978) and a 1978 reprint of Robert Frank's *The Americans* (1959), calling Hare's pictures of working people in their homes and workplaces and towns "devastating." Her review, "Slouching Towards Bethlehem, Pa.," is a nod to Joan Didion and a reference to Walker Evans's 1936 photographs of the town from within a cemetery and Hare's 1972 homage from almost the same spot — an improvement, in Malcolm's eyes. Hare had composed his picture around a graveyard angel, which seems to bow before a "menacingly bland reality." "He shows us to ourselves," Malcolm wrote, "as perhaps no other documentary photographer has ever done."

"We all thought he was crazy," Jack von Euw recently recalled of the day he met Chauncey Hare. He was speaking from his office at the Bancroft Library at the University of California, Berkeley, where he is curator of the pictorial collection, home to Hare's archives. "At that time I was an aspiring photographer and most of us would have given our left arm to be in that show. John was the kingmaker."

In 1979 Hare mailed a violently, if artfully defaced copy of *Mirrors and Windows* to Szarkowski's office, like a ransom note. He taped in sections of his protest pamphlet over some of the museum's text and collaged a Rosalind Fox Solomon photograph from the exhibition of a department store Santa below his own portrait of Orville England, transforming the page spread into a grim Christmas card ("Congratulations on the good work. All you 'friends' at MoMA. . . . Shafted again," he scrawled). He'd cut away the book's cover, and marked it up with references to those "friends," including Arthur Bullowa, a member of MoMA's Photography Committee and president of Aperture. Hare named one of the holes that he either cut or drilled through the center of the catalog a "Bullowa hole"—although it was probably not made by an actual bullet, it resembles the path of one, traveling through the pointer finger of a youth football player in a Richard P. Hume image, through the thigh of a girl in a plaid dress in a Helen Levitt photograph. It narrowly misses the crotch of a Key West sailor in a Marie Cosindas portrait but strikes the tire of an Eggleston farm truck, shatters the facade of a Stephen Shore building, the front yard of a Henry Wessel, Robert Adams's clear-cut Oregon forest, and finally lands on Lee Friedlander's trees. Whatever his implement—drill, awl, Exacto knife—Hare apparently meant to shoot straight through every mirror, every window.

When von Euw visited the exhibition that year, he found himself unsettled by the message delivered by Hare and also unable to ignore the presence of Philip Morris, whose name was boldly lettered on the gallery walls. "What did it mean that such a large corporation and one that merchandised cancer as a by-product should sponsor an art exhibition?" von Euw wrote decades later in the afterword to *Protest Photographs* (2009), Hare's third book. What seemed an act of self-sabotage in 1979 did not end Hare's photographic career—he would do that on his own terms—but it did illuminate the current of protest that arises from the core of his pictures. Von Euw tucked Hare's flier in his pocket and kept it for many years.

In all three books of photographs Hare published, he contributed a substantial and distinct autobiographical essay. His resistance to *Mirrors and Windows* is the defining moment of his life as a photographer; his awakening, though, occurred more than a decade prior, in March 1968, in Point Richmond, California. Point Richmond is under an hour's drive from Berkeley and the Haight, but a biopic of the turning point of Hare's life in the late '60s would not cue Jefferson Airplane or stock footage of flower children on acid. Chauncey Hare later wrote of meeting Orville England, who would become not only his most pivotal photographic subject but a close friend, "I was reminded of fairy tale gnomes who ask questions that may determine your fate." England, a stocky, genial man, approached Hare and asked if he wanted to buy a little plastic camera. How could this stranger have known, Hare wondered, that he had a Leica concealed in his jacket? He accompanied England and his wife Helen home.

Hare, an engineer at the Standard Oil Company, typically roamed the streets, camera in coat, on his lunch break. He had taken up photography much in the way he had taken up fishing, except in a few years' time he had gone from shyly shooting land-scapes and developing his film in a closet darkroom to making pictures not only with his Leica but also with a large-format view camera. He eventually learned that England, a refinery worker, had become disabled after being exposed to asbestos on the job. Hare's own grandfather had lost the use of a leg while working at Pittsburgh Steel. Objects and ephemera of England's home, which Hare returned to photograph the next day, evoked the concrete, household details Hare remembered from summers at his grandparents' house in Pennsylvania. If Hare was to eventually become the kind of photographer Szarkowski called a "window," Orville England was the mirror he needed, the reflection of his own life and the omen that would propel it forward. The photo-graph he made upon his return, of England sitting in his kitchen, was Hare's first real look into interior America.

Reproductions of Leonardo da Vinci's *The Last Supper* and paintings of horses and kittens and streams fill the rooms that Hare came to photograph in Pennsylvania, West Virginia, Ohio, the Sierra foothills, the San Francisco Bay Area, and places in between. Lamps, kettles, coffee cans, telephones, water heaters, blank televisions, and wall mirrors amplify the harrowing effect of his images. He rarely took more than one or two photographs at a time; he arrived bearing letters of recommendation from the Guggenheim Foundation and the Smithsonian, and came to experience what he called "magic" — "people expecting me when I had not met them before."

And yet, even when they are in a room together, Hare's subjects are revealed as utterly alone. In Wheeling, West Virginia, a husband and wife sit in separate armchairs, a child on each lap, like a pair of isolated islands adrift in a room crammed with doilies, plastic flowers, a collection of lanterns, and cheap art. The husband and wife wear television expressions, slack-jawed and stunned. "I've also discovered that by evening most of masculine Interior America is a little bit drunk," Hare wrote.

In his writings, Hare acknowledges the "deception" of using a wide-angle lens. Some subjects were not even aware they would appear in the frame, and definitely not imagining that certain details would creep into the picture: electric cords, dirty surfaces, windows and doors that opened onto other, dingier spaces. Sometimes Hare's camera is pitched to such a capacious angle that the apparent vastness of the room is terrifying. In other pictures, the camera's position lends itself to claustrophobic effect: floors recede into walls or wallpaper seems to swallow the carpet whole.

If there is a literary analogue, Hare's photographs might be a short story by Raymond Carver or Lucia Berlin. Hare discovers his decisive moment in the things no one wants him to see. "If anyone tries to keep me from looking somewhere, say, an upstairs bedroom," he wrote, "that's where I know I need to go." There might be an infant alone in a room. Or a man stalking through a boarding house, glaring at the camera. "You sonofabitch," he said to Hare. A telephone cord unwinds across the length of a living room, corralling the various family members. As Janet Malcolm observed, "In *Interior America*, Hare enters the homes that Frank sped past when taking the pictures for *The Americans*."

The spiritless worlds Hare discovered within them reflected his own life. Hare is descended from his paternal steelworker grandfather and a maternal grandfather who worked for the Shredded Wheat factory in Niagara Falls, New York. His mother, chronically depressed, spent days locked in her room. His father was an engineer who took pride in having an employee who washed his car for him. Hare's life proceeded in seemingly inevitable fashion: He went to engineering school at Columbia University without thinking much about it. He married his first wife, an Austrian waitress named Gertrude, without bothering to fall in love. He got his first job at Standard Oil (which became Chevron) in California without much trouble. A good recruiter, he noted in *Protest Photographs*, would have been suspicious of a company man who studied short stories at night.

At Chevron, Hare once worked with a team whose response to the nitrogen dioxide emanating from the refinery stacks was to recommend a way to render the gas colorless so that it would go undetected. Years in, his own invisible fears and unhappiness manifested in chronic nausea and vomiting. When he began photographing in the '60s, the symptoms disappeared. In 1969, Hare was granted leave from his job to travel the country in an Econoline van and photograph with his Guggenheim money. With subsequent Guggenheim grants, Hare earned permission to bring his camera into his own workplace, as well as into interiors of other corporations. "He took on the hardest subject there was," recalls Bill Owens, who was then making the pictures that would become *Suburbia* (1973). "Ordinary people doing ordinary work in ordinary offices."

Hare's fight to publish *This Was Corporate America* in 1984 triggered a period that he describes as cutting ties with the photography and art world. "Each photograph had become a record of promise I had taken on," he wrote, and to sell those records, or to show them as purely aesthetic images, he believed, would have been tantamount to selling the people.

Ken Light, who was making photographs of industrial workers when he first met Hare in the early 1980s, corresponded with him for years. "He felt a complete responsibility to the people he photographed, and wanting to change the world or change their status and I think that's why he gave it up," Light said recently. "With *Interior America*, people thought he was the new Walker

Evans. But Evans was very disconnected from the people he photographed. He was interested in the image, the actual object. And Chauncey was this wonderful photographer for whom the photograph wasn't enough. He cared about the people."

After divorcing Gertrude, and giving up custody of their son, Victor, Hare eventually moved in with Orville and Helen, caring for them until Orville's death. He immersed himself in the life of one of the prostitutes he photographed, and tried to help her beat a heroin addiction. He began attending what he described as "meet-members-of-the-opposite-sex" parties on Saturday nights and "newspaper dating." Mostly he went out with psychotherapists and psychologists; he baked them apple pies. When Judy Wyatt, a therapist, answered a personal ad in the *San Francisco Bay Guardian*, she found herself meeting a "wiry man, compact, handsome in a falcon-like way, wearing light-blue corduroy bell-bottoms and a jacket. There was a tense, imploded energy running stiff through him—a little frightening." And yet, there was an instant spark between them. The next day, Hare called Wyatt and told her, "You are the one." "Our values were a perfect match," he later wrote. They fell in love, and into lifelong collaboration.

After they were married, Hare got a series of degrees—an MFA from the San Francisco Art Institute, and an MA in organizational development from Pepperdine University, completing his thesis on employee morale at the US Environmental Protection Agency, where he was then working. Several months into the job, an EPA worker, who had been hired at the same time as Hare, leapt from a nearby building to his death. Hare was eventually fired when the agency got wind of his morale survey. During one of their vacations to Yosemite, Wyatt coined the term "work abuse," and she and Hare, who became a licensed therapist himself, began dedicating their professional lives to counseling people traumatized by their jobs. They published a book, *Work Abuse: How to Recognize and Survive It* (1997), and they maintained a private practice in San Francisco. (Hare died in 2019.)

One day in 1999, Jack von Euw picked up his phone and heard at the other end of the line the man he'd seen picketing his own art exhibition twenty years before. "It was as if I had received a ransom call," von Euw wrote. Hare was looking to donate his photographs, but on very specific terms. The work could not be sold; the work could not leave the library; the work could not be shown out of context—hence the statement that must always accompany the publication of his photographs. If the Bancroft Library didn't agree to Hare's conditions, well, von Euw was certain that Chauncey Hare's entire photographic record was destined for a bonfire. He agreed to meet Hare at a warehouse in Oakland with a flashlight, old clothes, and a large screwdriver. What he found was astounding: a massive collection of prints, negatives, books, accumulations of everything that represented Hare's life as a photographer. "In my view his work is unparalleled," von Euw recounted. "You'd have to go back to the days of the Farm Security Administration. Chauncey is a writer, but he writes with his camera. I can't think of another photographer who is as closely related to writing as he is except maybe Eugene Smith. And his photographs have never been more relevant than they are now."

Hare was able to get up close to the riders on their BART commutes, he once said, simply because he was fueled by rage, an emotion that, along with severe anxiety, is what continually motivated his work. The aim was always something that lay beyond the offices and kitchens of the lives he encountered: "My photographs," he wrote, "demand a spiritual awakening."

Originally published in *Aperture*, issue 226, "American Destiny," Spring 2017.

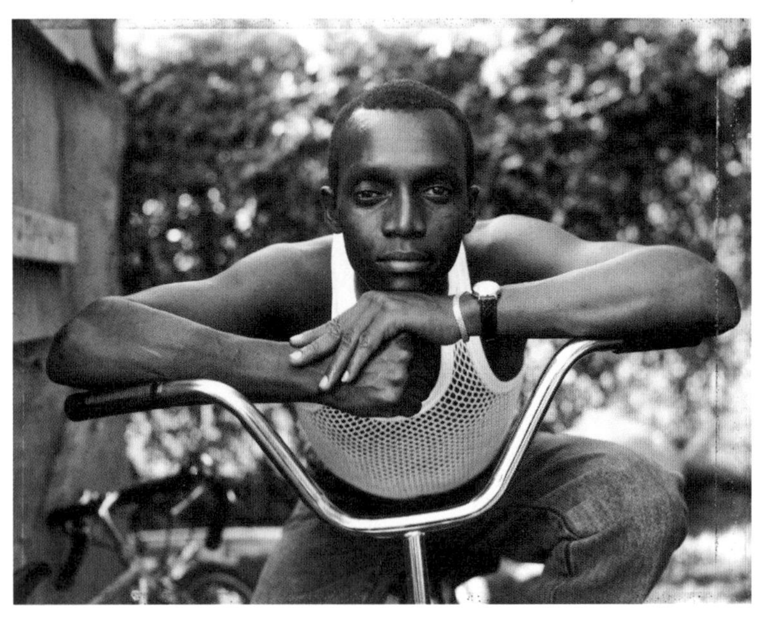

Dawoud Bey, *A Young Man Resting on an Exercise Bike, Amityville, NY*, 1988

Picturing the Past-Present: A Visit with Dawoud Bey in Brooklyn

The apartment house on Cambridge Place in Clinton Hill is quintessentially Brooklyn, a stately foundation propping up faded pale brick, with curved bow windows and wrought iron detailing on its fence and front door, seemingly unchanged for years. Its wide stoop has a vantage onto a lively swath of Fulton Street, the destination and origin of much of its foot traffic. From 1978 to 1991, those coming and going included preteens striking a pose in overalls, bookish young boys, young MCs and track stars, little girls in Sunday dress, men and women headed to the cleaner, the barber, the bodega. During those years the artist Dawoud Bey observed this steady flow of everyday Black beauty, occasionally pulling a face out of the crowd to make a picture with his Polaroid Type 55 camera. He photographed in close proximity, usually with very few background details, and printed large, in luminous black and white tones, so that one can look directly into the eyes of Bey's friends and neighbors. The pictures, Hilton Als has written, "conveyed the satisfaction of being seen, which is a form of brotherhood and love, too."

On a recent afternoon, we met on those steps. Bey was in town from his longtime home in Chicago for the installation and opening of *Dawoud Bey: An American Project*, his career retrospective at the Whitney Museum of American Art. The exhibition, which previously opened at the San Francisco Museum of Modern Art in February 2020 before moving to the High Museum in Atlanta, spans a period when his photographs had an easier time traveling than their maker. After and amid months of grief and isolation, the communal gaze in his portraits resonates deeply but, more important, its eight distinct bodies of work, made over forty-six years, also offer the opportunity to simultaneously slip through multiple eras of time. If the subjects on view—from Harlem street scenes to the shadow realm of the Underground Railroad—feel particularly prescient, clarifying, and challenging, it's because Bey has always been speaking to the current moment, imaginatively questioning the past and its place in our experience of the now.

Bey was perched on his old stoop, wearing a dark red corduroy blazer over a printed button-down shirt, jeans, and loafers— as innately stylish as the people in his pictures. We had pulled down our masks to talk. The sun was out, the air was moving, and Bey, who began wearing a hearing aid in grade school, is used to reading lips. We looked together through the just-published *Street Portraits*. "Initially it has to come from a real interest in the subject," Bey said. "You can't fake that. Richard Avedon said, All the photographs I make, they're really portraits of me. And people said, That arrogant bastard!" He laughed. "But I believe it. If it's not in you, there's no real way to communicate that. They only look the way they do because it's my photograph. In another picture, Sunshine Bracey might be smiling. I'm not interested in the exterior smile, that kind of public presentation we've come to expect. I was always interested in interiority." A particular marvel of Bey's work is that, even when it comes to his youngest subjects, his portraits vividly reveal this quality. "They were complex people, and there was a rich interiority that inhabited them."

In Clinton Hill in the 1980s, Bey had been thinking about Avedon's *American West* portraits, especially the way, made against spare backdrops, they depended greatly on gestural language. Bey wouldn't work in a studio until 1991, when he moved away to enter the Yale MFA photography program as a thirty-eight-year-old artist and new father. But in Brooklyn, he had already worked through similar constraints. "Place a dude in front of a camera, and how do you make it nuanced?" he said. "And, of course, I'm wrapping all those histories and ideas around the idea of the Black subject. Avedon's in the studio with Marilyn Monroe and whoever. I'm out here in the street with these folks! But I had an acute awareness of that history and I wanted to have a conversation with that history."

Born David Edward Smikle and raised in Jamaica, Queens, Bey started out as an aspiring drummer, studying with his neighbor, the jazz pioneer Milford Graves. Bey began making his first significant photographs in the early 1970s, around the time when he began using his chosen name. In Harlem, a neighborhood where his family maintained strong connections and the cultural territory of many of his core influences, he worked in the 35mm tradition of the great street photographers. He initially aimed for "'positive' pictures of the Black community," a notion he soon dismantled as counterproductive.

"There's a man standing there talking to his friends—but is that 'positive'? I quickly realized that didn't work," Bey told me. "It wasn't *useful* to the complex thing of taking in the world and the people in it and shaping it into photographs." Instead, as if adding to a dialogue begun by his artistic predecessor Roy DeCarava, Bey's camera found a tender and complicated realism in the contemporary life of the neighborhood and its people. Bey's first major solo show took place at the Studio Museum of Harlem in 1979. "Ultimately, Bey represents Harlem as a state of mind," the artist and historian Deborah Willis wrote in *Seeing Deeply*, a 2018 collection of his works.

Intellectually, the next phase of his work came from a nagging impulse. "One of the things that I intentionally wanted to do was make pictures on the block that I lived on," he said, nodding in the direction of Fulton Street. "I was always packing my camera and going someplace else. I began to think about that." He pointed to a photograph of a bearded man with a wizened face—Peg, who set up a shoeshine stand on the corner. "He was like the neighborhood sage. He kind of *looks* like a sage," Bey said, recalling the group of older men who would congregate, hang out all day. He laughed. "And you know, this is the interesting thing: I don't know if I ever saw him actually shining anybody's shoes."

Peg and his polish and brushes are long gone from the corner, but former neighbors spill in and out of the apartment building. "Is that who I think it is under that mask?" Bey said to a woman gingerly carrying out her recycling. One parcel tumbled from her grasp as she recognized him. "Dawoud, is that you?!" This turned out to be Lolita, Bey's instantly charismatic former landlady, who, moments earlier, he had compared to Alice B. Toklas, for her salon-like relationship to the artists who rented from her, many drawn there by the proximity to Pratt Institute. "We had it going *on*," Lolita affirmed, settling down on the opposite step. "This building *rocked*." It was through his friends, artist Marilyn Nance and filmmaker Al Santana, that Bey heard of a vacant apartment, with a starting rent of $175. He was astonished to learn that most of his old neighbors still live here.

A block away, now, there are murals in honor of Biggie Smalls, born on St. James Place, which was recently rechristened Christopher "Notorious B.I.G." Wallace Way. Bey never photographed him. "Biggie was always in hardcore mode when he was in the streets," he said. Kids from Junior M.A.F.I.A., a group of rappers mentored by Wallace, shared an apartment down the block; they were younger and more approachable. "I could talk to them," Bey said. "They were just hanging around Biggie, trying to get some of that reflective whatever-it-was they thought he had coming off of him." He asked Lolita if she knew what had become of the teenage girl depicted on the back of *Street Portraits*, her track medals pinned to her shirt. "I always hoped that would become the shape of her life."

Lolita looked through other pictures. "Ooh! That's Bracey," she said. "Ooh! That's a good one too." She and Bey enumerated some of the intervening changes in Brooklyn: Condos have replaced the Board of Education in downtown Brooklyn, for instance. "Used

     PICTURING THE PAST-PRESENT

to be," he began, "when you said 110 Livingston, you meant—"
and Lolita quickly finished, "—the Board of Ed!"

Even Bey's mention of the Board of Education felt tethered
to his work. It calls to mind his project *Harlem Redux*, a provoca-
tive depiction of the neighborhood in the midst of gentrification.
It also reflects the way he has steadily pursued his own artistic
growth while simultaneously seeking out meaningful teaching and
art-making projects with museums and institutions. Through this
way of working, he began to nudge the portrait into a collaborative
space, with the formal, large-scale color photographs in his *Class
Pictures* series (1992–2007). This questioning the shape of a young
person's life would point him, eventually, to Birmingham, Alabama.

Bey's upbringing in Queens was middle-class and socially
conscious. In 1964, a year after four girls were killed in the
white supremacist bombing of the 16th Street Baptist Church in
Birmingham, Alabama, his parents went to see James Baldwin
lecture at Calvary Baptist Church in Jamaica. They came home
with a copy of *The Movement* by Lorraine Hansberry and SNCC,
illustrated with photographs. Bey, then eleven, absorbed the
picture of twelve-year-old Sarah Jean Collins, severely wounded
in the attack that killed her sister Addie Mae, Cynthia Wesley,
Denise McNair, and Carole Robertson. Decades later Bey would
bolt upright in bed one night, suddenly seized by the memory of
the photograph.

In the early 2000s, while still making *Class Pictures*, Bey
began to make exploratory visits to Birmingham, where he
learned from local archives that two Black boys, Virgil Ware and
Johnny Robinson, had also been killed in racial violence that day.
"I didn't even know about the boys, but the four girls had such
a mythic presence. I wanted to make it palpable." He made portraits
of local girls and boys who were the same ages as the six children
had been when they were killed, yet to Bey they still did not fully
convey precisely what had haunted him. "I realized I was trying to
visualize 'the past' and the past of their lives without figuring out
the other important piece of it, which was *what* it was and *who*

it was they never got to become because of that moment." He made photographs of adults who had lived through the terror and paired their portraits with those of the children, side by side. In these diptychs, what becomes visible is time, both a gulf between the two and a connection—survived time, lived time, stolen time, the future time in the lives of the younger generation.

At the Whitney, the *Birmingham Project* is shown separately from the rest of the retrospective, in an enclosed first-floor gallery that has the feel of a small sanctuary, the photographs like chapel windows. In the dual-channel video *9.15.63*, scored to music by Bey's son, Ramon Alvarez-Smikle, one camera pans over the brushes and chairs of an empty barbershop and drawings by little kids, while the other grazes gently through trees, rooftops, and, finally, the steeple and stained glass windows of the 16th Street Baptist Church.

"That was a conceptual breakthrough for me," Bey said. "That's when I decided to continue history-based work. All the issues that have to do with that history are still being played out now, and they have their basis in that formative relationship with enslaved Africans being brought over here—not to be fully participating social citizens but to be used as enslaved labor and drive the economy. They were expendable, very much in the way that Black people in certain circumstances continue to be expendable." He spoke from his stoop three days after the police killing of Daunte Wright in Minnesota, during the third week in the trial of Derek Chauvin.

"George Floyd was viewed as expendable," Bey continued emphatically. "That Minneapolis officer had no more regard for George Floyd's life than a slavedriver would have had in 1750. It is a complete disregard and a dehumanization of Black life that begins with the institution of slavery and the site itself, which is the plantation. I thought I needed to go to those places to bear witness, but also to construct a representation of what it means."

The last room of the exhibition contains nine photographs from the first series of his current three-part project. *Night Coming*

Tenderly, Black, was made in Ohio, showing the landscape of purported stops along the Underground Railroad from the vantage of an unseen fugitive at night. "When I started thinking about the blackness of the subject in a photograph moving through the blackness of space, that's Roy DeCarava in a very singular way," Bey said. He consciously applied the way DeCarava radically portrayed Black skin in gloriously darkened tones to his unpeopled landscapes; Bey photographed them during the day and printed them dark. "It was meant to be a materially beautiful space." The title, from Langston Hughes's poem "Dream Variations," merged intrinsically: "While night comes on gently, Dark like me — That is my dream!"

Bey intends the pictures to envelop. Stand before them and, slowly, your eyes will adjust, looking below trees, along fences, remaining alert to present dangers, whether the white farmhouse in the distance is menace or friend. Look longer, and another world of tones and details emerge, reveling in the obscure and the sense of being hidden, the forests and yards and the vast great lake and the night itself forming a protective cloak and an alternate world—a dream.

The landscapes are mostly oblique, resonant with evocative, timeless details: the curve of a picket fence, the cover of a tree. At the same time there are anachronistic interruptions—what appears to be an air conditioner in one window, for instance, as if to remind the viewer that the past lives on. In the grammar of time, "past-present" is the natural state of Bey's pictures, a term he uses himself. "I reinscribe the past in the space of the photograph," he said.

After the Whitney exhibition, he will return to Louisiana to resume *In This Here Place*, the next phase of the series that was disrupted by the pandemic, including a color video triptych, *Evergreen,* in which trees bear vigilant witness to the empty plantation of its setting, and photographing across several more plantations. These pictures require a different treatment, Bey said, "to allow the viewer to believe as if they are physically inhabiting these spaces in time, to see and feel every detail, materially, viscerally."

The final stop for this series inevitably draws him to the origins of enslaved Africans in America: Virginia. As always, he will be guided by research, but not encumbered by it. "I think about a writer like Toni Morrison, who wrote epic fiction that is based on real history but it's not a mere retelling of it," Bey said. "It's using that history to create something that's rooted in it, amplifying it through this rigorous kind of reimagining, and being adept enough at the craft to shape it into something credible. So that people believe it. And not just believe in it, but are moved by it."

One day in 2019, when *Night Coming Tenderly, Black* was first shown at the Art Institute of Chicago, Bey walked into the gallery with a friend, and two visitors looked away from the photographs, startled to recognize the artist among his own images. "They said, 'But *you made* these,'" he recalled. "They were so deep in the liminal space between past and present, exactly where I wanted them to be."

Originally published on Vanity Fair online on April 22, 2021.

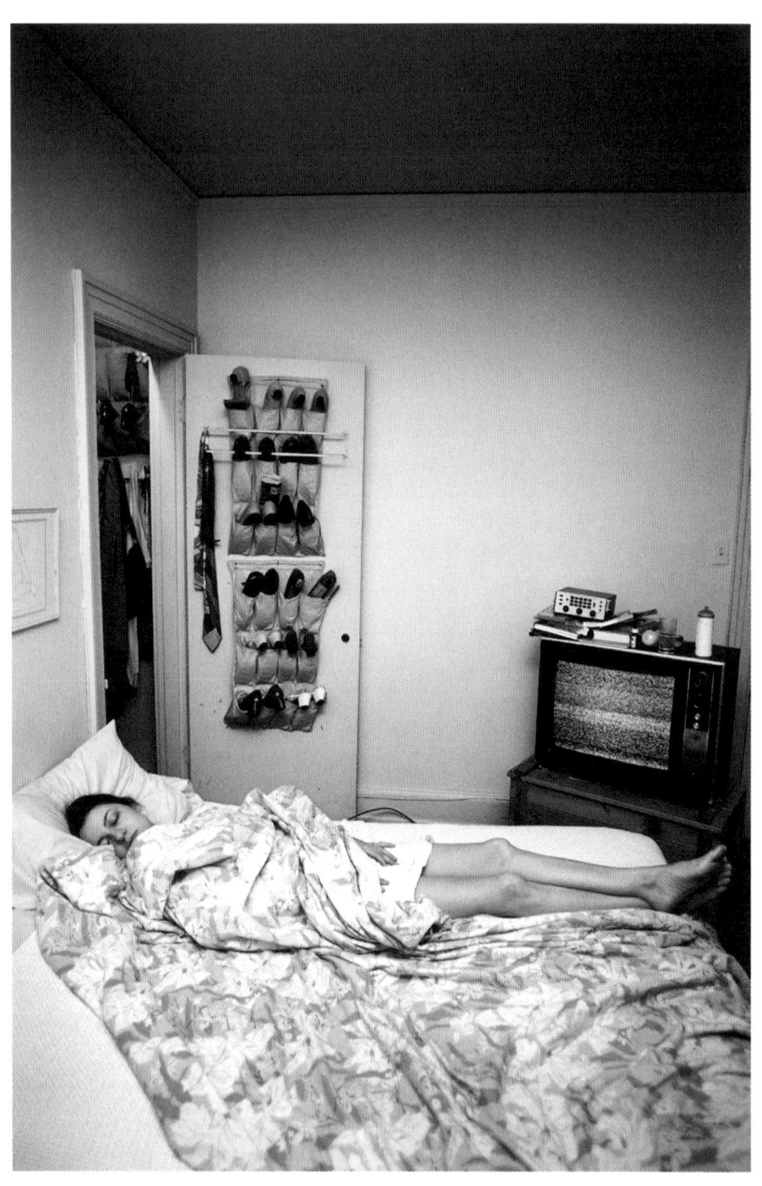

William Eggleston, *Untitled*, ca. 1971

Strange Hours:
William Eggleston in Memphis,
William Eggleston in New York City

MEMPHIS, 2008

"*Bill Eggleston* has a show at the *Whitney*?" asks a woman at the bar inside the Lamplighter Lounge in Memphis. She practically spits out her Budweiser. "I hate his shit!" Sam Cooke is on the jukebox, which plays real 45s; placemats are spread along the wood veneer, and the complimentary matchbooks are from D&D Bail Bonds in Wichita Falls, Texas. The bartender, Shirley, slices potatoes in the kitchen. A young couple are making out at a back table.

"I'm from the same town as him," says another woman, who hails from Sumner, Mississippi. "I know his cousin Maudie. She's a photographer too."

"I like Weegee's photographs," the first woman cuts in. And again: "Bill Eggleston at the *Whitney*?"

There's a snapshot of William Eggleston at the back of the Lamp, displayed by a vase of unnaturally colored silk flowers, a dish of peppermints, and a cutout of James Dean. The arrangement itself is prime material for an Eggleston photograph. In fact, earlier that day, the Lamp turns up in a box of proofs at the Eggleston Artistic Trust. There in supersaturated color is the bar's EAT MORE POSSUM sign.

Eggleston has a precarious relationship with the Lamp, one of his favorite haunts. In fact, he's barred from entering. "I got really drunk one time," he tells me, "and I threw a hamburger at Shirley, who had just made it. But we're still friends."

Shirley had been fond but firm: "He calls me up every now and then, asks how I'm doing, and I say, 'Good.'" She is pleased to own an Eggleston photograph at home and proud of his success, but, like the Lamp's regulars, her feelings for her famous neighbor are complicated. "I like Bill, but he can't come in here. Will you be sure and tell him I said hello?"

The consummate insider-outsider, Eggleston remains aloof in the numerous worlds he inhabits—intricate relationships that will be on full display at the Whitney when his first comprehensive retrospective, *William Eggleston: Democratic Camera*, opens Friday—his most prominent return to the city since his MoMA debut in 1976.*

We meet at the offices of his archive, a few miles east of the Lamp. He's dressed sharp as ever: off-white lace-up oxfords, dark tailored pants, an undone bow tie over a blue oxford shirt monogrammed with a large orange *B*. "Got it at a yard sale. It had my name on it: B, for Bill." He laughs. Eggleston has been known to wear knee-high Austrian riding boots and, according to Lamp regulars, "Zorro capes." "Sometimes, yes," he confirms. "It's comfortable, and it looks good."

In 1967, when Eggleston arrived in New York from Memphis bearing a box of slides that would redefine photography, he was an anomaly. Not only was he one of the first serious photographers to wholeheartedly embrace color, but he embraced exactly what made color photography so controversial in highbrow circles: He treated the commonplace as art. He calls it photographing "democratically," meaning anything—parking lots, shopping centers—was a worthy subject. "I thought I was doing the right thing, put it that way," he says now. "And if someone told me something otherwise, I just put it aside."

He was soon befriended by what he calls a small "club" of artists—Diane Arbus, Lee Friedlander, and Garry Winogrand. "Though our work was different, we felt that we were compatriots,"

                                              STRANGE HOURS

Eggleston says. "Somehow I knew we were, attitude-wise, doing the same thing."

Scorned at the time for being "vulgar" and "banal," Eggleston's 1976 MoMA exhibition has since been revered for exactly those reasons. It was accompanied by a cheekily titled book, *William Eggleston's Guide*, misread by many as an artistic travelogue to his native South. In truth, it was a Michelin guide to Eggleston's heightened way of seeing: His use of supernatural dye-transfer color, which implied that the ordinary was not at all so. His startling compositions directed viewers to look as closely as his camera, to recognize the grace, violence, and humor implicit in the mundane. A tricycle that appeared as tall and magnificent as a Cadillac. A fire burning in a barbecue grill. A red ceiling, bright as fresh blood.

The New York art world became fascinated with Eggleston's Southernness, and he, in turn, immersed himself in the scene, setting up house in the Chelsea Hotel with Warhol star Viva for a time. But he maintained a life in Memphis and a marriage to his wife, Rosa Dossett Eggleston (with whom he had three children), while openly having other relationships.

Evidence of this double life shows up in the Whitney retrospective, which features the museum premiere of Eggleston's foray into filmmaking. *Stranded in Canton* (the last syllable pronounced like *tone*), is a full-length video vérité, shot around 1975 in New Orleans and Memphis and navigating a seventies Delta netherworld of quaalude-popping dentists, a soliloquizing collaborator, Randall, whom Eggleston also referred to as "Dr. Reflecto," cryptologists, bluesmen—a Southern equivalent of the Chelsea. Eggleston wanted it all to flow "like a symphony." His parallel lives, he says, are necessary: "It does get confusing sometimes. But each of these things allows the other. It creates a state of mind."

In 1983, Priscilla Presley commissioned Eggleston to photograph the Graceland mansion, which had only recently reopened to the public after Elvis's death in 1977. "She asked me if I'd mind not photographing certain places, one of which was the death bedroom and bathroom," he recalls. "I said, not a bit, Priscilla, you just tell me—in fact, I'll just restrict my pictures to the downstairs because that's the real Graceland. That's the one people know about and see." It is perhaps his most essentially Memphis series, and the most daunting.

"That Graceland project, it was the most difficult one I've ever done," Eggleston ventures. He worked nights, arriving after the gates closed to visitors, over a period of two and a half months. "Sometimes I spent an entire night till dawn and never could figure out a certain picture to take. And then I'd come back the next night . . . And it was pretty spooky, I was the only person in the house."

He exaggerated only a little. Sometimes his son Winston had assisted him, trailing long extension cords and floodlights. Eggleston recalls bringing a tripod for the long exposures he made with a 35mm and a 6-by-9 camera. Once in a while they ran into Elvis's Aunt Delta. "And sometimes during the night a brace of maids would come in to thoroughly clean for the next day and it would take them an hour or more. And they swore, each one of them, that they saw Elvis's ghost. And they were serious." Which Elvis did they see? I wonder. He was a sleepwalker, after all, who reportedly kept his bedroom ice cold. Eggleston laughs a little, and repeats their account, equal parts *Mystery Train* and *Scooby-Doo*. "That's all they said. There's a painting of Elvis that's in one of the photographs and they swore that it would move. He would move in the painting, or something." Much later, I'm reminded of a scene in Don DeLillo's *White Noise*, in which the character Babette reads aloud from a series of tabloid predictions: "The ghost of Elvis Presley will be seen taking lonely walks at dawn around Graceland, his musical mansion."

Eggleston photographed Elvis's gold-leaf-encrusted piano, his statue of a white monkey with its little nails painted black, the mirrors reflecting portraits of Elvis, the mirrors reflecting other mirrors, the gold and sea blue and patterned drapes completely obscuring the windows. Writing in *Artforum* in 1984, Greil Marcus described the Graceland pictures as "a 1957–77 version of King Tut's tomb." Elvis, Richard Harrington wrote that year in the *Washington Post*, "is revealed as much in his absence as he was by his presence. This was his home, the realization of his empty dreams, his proof against the night." In one frame, Eggleston photographed from inside the locked iron gates, ornamented with angels and guitars, looking out across Elvis Presley Boulevard—toward the lonesome glow of commercial fluorescence against a purple twilight sky.

The Whitney retrospective demonstrates Eggleston's mastery in depicting the place of a place. But it is equally possible to see the show as just the opposite: a career-long meditation on how the particular can reveal the abstract—the composition of light and its reflection.

It's four o'clock, and Eggleston, sitting on the stoop outside his office, smokes another in a long line of cigarettes. The late sun striking the cars in the lot recalls his first real color photograph: a bag boy pushing a row of carts. "This is beginning to be my favorite kind of light," he remarks.

A week or so later, when I am back in New York, we speak on the phone. Eggleston says he'd hoped I would have called him up to go back to the Lamp and I can't tell if he is joking or not. He'd spent the rest of that night staying up late playing music instead. "I keep strange hours, I guess," he reckons. I agree—I am not just thinking of the way he struck me as someone who belongs to the day and night pretty equally, but also about how his photographs reveal such a surreal awareness of the way that light moves and changes, about how they are of all times, all lights. I mention the Graceland photos again.

"Those were done with artificial light," Eggleston emphasizes. "Although you couldn't tell. Elvis kept the drapes pulled, these big heavy drapes, whether it was day or night. Elvis kept strange hours too."

He speaks as he had when we were in Memphis on that stoop, as if he were finishing the same cigarette, his words precise, elegantly drawn out. "You know, the only light I don't care for is at noon when it's straight down," he says. "When we were talking the other day it was just about exactly four and that is my favorite time or even an hour or so later. The light at that time brings out a spectrum that appeals to me, colors that I think are there but I just don't always notice in other lights. It's like when a thunderstorm moves through and the light changes swiftly from cold to warm."

NEW YORK CITY, 2017

In 1976, William Eggleston made the pictures that would become his portfolio *Election Eve*, a road trip from his home in Memphis to Jimmy Carter's hometown of Plains, Georgia. He avoided, to paraphrase his famous quote, the obvious, and veered off the campaign trail, with its barber shops and town halls and babies to be kissed; instead he photographed emptied yards, sides of barns, churches with hand-painted names in crooked lettering, weeds poking through red Georgia clay. His pictures did not require human beings. I first saw some of the images that make up *Election Eve* around the time of Bush vs. Gore, and I have not trusted a poll since. The real signs, as they do with much of Eggleston's work, lie in the landscape.

I went to meet him a week before the presidential election. In a room at the Bowery Hotel he sat in a loveseat and asked, in his low register, if I would sit by him. His daughter, Andra, who designs textiles based on her father's drawings, would soon join us. Eggleston's Leica rested on a coffee table, next to a glass of water and an ashtray. CNN played on the television, but nobody in the room paid any attention to it, least of all Eggleston, who has steadfastly expressed disinterest in politics for as long as he has been giving interviews.

He wore a suit and an ascot tie, half undone, presumably for no particular reason other than the fact that he nearly always wears one. He claims to have never owned a pair of jeans. He was

    STRANGE HOURS

jacket-less, perfectly tailored, shoes shined. It was just the way
he was dressed eight years ago in Memphis, when I first met him
before his major retrospective at the Whitney Museum, and it was
the way he had been dressed the previous evening at an Aperture
gala, "Dear Bill," at which he was the guest of honor. He had not,
I had noticed, stuck around long enough to hear "Nature Boy,"
a song that was sung as a tribute to him. It was perfectly all right,
we decided, that he had cut out a little early; after all, he had quite
a lot going that week in New York, and for a good while to come.
This was the eve, too, of his exhibition, *The Democratic Forest*,
at the David Zwirner gallery, which began representing him late
last year. The show featured a selection of new photographs from
his epic series of some 1,500 photographs made between 1983
and 1986. In the '80s, Eggleston described the project this way:
"Friends would ask what I was doing and I would tell them that
I was working on a project with several thousand prints. They
would laugh but I would be dead serious. At least I had found
a friend in that title, *The Democratic Forest*, that would look
over me."

Democratic, referring not to the Party, but to an equanimity of
subject. If his 1976 Museum of Modern Art debut legitimized color
photography as art, the shelter of the title *Democratic Forest* gave
him permission to go everywhere, beginning with the cotton fields
of his native Mississippi and prowling the back lots and side roads
and lost corners of the American South, Pittsburgh, Berlin, and
elsewhere. In his hands, the camera becomes a palpable, itinerant
presence; the scope feels restless, filmic. Nothing was off-limits,
and nothing mattered more than anything else. The image of
a child's face—even the face of his own child—carried no more
photographic weight than a rusted car door. That car door could
be freighted with just as much feeling as one of the luminous
large-format portraits: artistically, Eggleston approached and
treated them the same. His places and objects are attitudinally
akin to a Cézanne still life, and frequently more autobiographically
revelatory than his people. Place is central to Eggleston, and no

junkyard, no field, no food stand, no porch, no laundry room can be viewed as insignificant.

The *Democratic Forest* exhibit was accompanied by a new edition of his book of the same name, and it was preceded in late 2015 by publication of a monumental ten-volume set of the series, and it came on the heels of *William Eggleston: Portraits*, at the National Gallery in London, which travels to Australia next month, accompanied by a new catalog. Another exhibition, *Los Alamos*, opens at Foam in Amsterdam in March. As sprawling as *The Democratic Forest*, it is made up of works shot on subsequent travels throughout the American South and West, including, as its title indicates, the town in New Mexico where the nuclear bomb was developed in secret.

If this sounds like an awful lot of Eggleston pictures resurfacing in the world, well, it is. It's difficult, at least in my own world, to find someone who has never seen them before. But to look at his photographs again, especially now, and even the ones you think you know well, is to induce a fresh vision. In her introduction to the original edition of *The Democratic Forest*, Eggleston's dear friend Eudora Welty wrote what remains the wisest and most astute thing that has ever been written about his work. This was in 1989, and rings louder now still:

> Our own way of seeing may have recently been in trouble. These days, not only the world that we look out upon but the human eye itself seems at times occluded, as if a cataract had thickened over it from within. We have become used to what we live with, caloused [sic] (perhaps in self-protection) to what's happened outside our door, and we now accept its worsening. But Eggleston's vision of the world is clear, and clarifying to our own.

At the hotel, Eggleston and I looked through some of his photographs together. "That looks like New Orleans," he said, at a picture in which only parts of street corners or houses were visible.

It was architectural, he suggested, but it was something else too. I reminded him that the last time we met, he told me that when he gets his printer's proofs, he first looks at them upside down. "This is true," he said. "You see things in there that you wouldn't normally see." We examined a photograph of an auto shop and car wash ("a very complicated composition," he declared), turning it this way and that. Electric wires and poles bisect the frame; arrows point to its outer edges; signs jut into cars, into asphalt, directing attention everywhere.

Elsewhere in the room, his friend the artist Leanna Hicks sat on a bed, crouched over a little black book, in which she was painting fantastical, saturated scenes in acrylic and enamels, scenes with titles like *Matilda Waiting in Hell* and *Lucinda in the Apex*. She was introduced to Eggleston several years ago through a mutual friend. "I didn't know his photographs then," she told me. She had just moved to Memphis from Louisiana. "When I walked in the door, I was like, who are you? And he was like, who are *you?*" She laughed. "Coming where I come from, I don't think anybody's a big deal," Hicks continued. "But now he's one of my best friends. He's unapologetic. You know, the minute you submit your will to somebody else's opinion, a piece of you dies. You got to believe in yourself wholeheartedly. Some people might interpret that as ruthless but I think that's living a good life."

Living a good life is central to understanding Eggleston, whose patience for convention and dull moments is slim, and who has as strong an appetite for the company of women as he does for an eccentric, fun-loving crowd of associates. He managed to layer that life onto the one he lived with his wife of fifty years, the beautiful, forceful, and literary-minded Rosa; she died in the summer of 2015.

Though they were based mostly in Memphis, Eggleston willfully rejects the tag "Southern photographer"; he once told a reporter he prefers "citizen of the world."

And why not? Eggleston has also lived often in New York and in Paris, the city of his great hero Henri Cartier-Bresson as well as in the New Orleans and Delta late nights of *Stranded in Canton*. When he was commissioned to photograph his friends Gus van Sant and David Byrne's movies, he went off and made pictures of the world of the films instead ("Sets are boring," he declared). He is a fine piano player who began playing when he was four—"like Mozart!" he told me. His favorite composer is Bach.

"I truly believe that if you look at his drawings and listen to the music my father listens to, you will gain a better understanding of him as an artist," Andra told me that afternoon. She wore a bright agnès b. dress made from one of her Electra Eggleston patterns based on one of her father's drawings, and a new pair of Christian Louboutin stiletto boots. Her brother, William III, edited the recent volumes of *The Democratic Forest*; with their brother Winston, they direct the archives of the Eggleston Trust. Andra rarely connected with her father's photographs. She gravitated instead, she said, to his piano playing, and to the vivid, abstract drawings he has made for years, often with Sharpie, and frequently on hotel stationery. Recently she had a memory of how her father used to retrieve the patterns that, as a child, she would draw and toss in the wastebasket; in the morning she'd discover them pinned up on the wall. A few years ago, she began salvaging her father's sketches and turning them into textile patterns.

The room was chilly; she pointed to a black overcoat thrown over a chair. "Is that yours, Dad?"

"It's old Gaultier," Eggleston said.

"Paris!" Andra wrapped it around her shoulders.

"I think my greatest experience in watching my dad photograph was being witness to the way he saw things," Andra said. "I used to watch him study things—something so ordinary and so seemingly simple. Like there would be a set of glasses that had no monetary value and he would zoom in on those glasses and study them, visually, for sometimes days. And that was the object of his intention. And it drove my mother crazy! But that, I think, was the greatest gift my dad has given me, to be able to see that."

I wondered when it had become apparent to her that her father was an artist. "It was sort of difficult and scary for me to understand what he was and who he was," Andra said. "There was a lot of drama growing up. It was certainly quite unconventional. It just comes with the territory. You know, he doesn't exactly photograph the *wilderness*" — Hicks, who was still painting in her sketchbook, laughed loudly at this, and so did Andra — "I mean he wasn't just peeking in on the situation, he was living that situation . . ."

"Like the brick?" I asked. In a recent segment on *CBS Sunday Morning*, she had described a brick being thrown through the window of their family home, ostensibly by one of her father's girlfriends.

"Oh yes," Eggleston said in an offhand way.

"You know," Andra said, "there's another part of that story, which is that one night my mom got really pissed off and decided she was going to dress up like my dad and go over to his girlfriend's house with a brick; she was clearly inspired by the brick-through-the-window incident."

"Now that I don't recall," Eggleston said dryly.

"Winston told me the other night! He said he clearly remembered her putting on khaki pants and a white-button down shirt and she was all revved up to go over to her house and throw a brick. I don't know that she actually went over there and did it, but it was more the magic of thinking about that."

I had seen Rosa in Eggleston's photographs, in Michael Almereyda's documentary, *William Eggleston in the Real World*, and heard some of the family stories, and it was enough to make me wish aloud that I'd had the chance to meet her. "I wish you had too," Eggleston said, with extra gravity. "She had an incredible eye. She always knew if a photograph of mine was good or not. She was always right. It was" — he paused — "*inescapable* not to notice how correct she always was."

What may very well come off to some as indifference — considering a person or a crack in the sidewalk as photographic equals — is actually a more enlightened sort of vision. In its own way, it is the noblest political act for a man who claims to exist outside of politics: What he has perfected in his photographs is a way of seeing without judgment. Now it struck me that his way of looking is the visual equivalent of deep, intent listening.

"Do you still play piano every day?" I asked him.

"Yes," he answered, "and into the night."

"Do you record it? Do people record you?"

"No," he said. "It's a lot of trouble to set it up. I live in an apartment building that was once a hotel. Rosa and I started living there the day after we were married. Didn't have any children, didn't need a house. We spent a lot of time growing up with my parents outside in the country, which means a cotton plantation. I held onto the apartment all these years. I just go in and instantly start playing. I listen very intently to what's coming out of the piano."

What had spoken to him, I wondered, the first time he heard Bach.

"I think the best word is *abstract*," Eggleston said. "Bach was not trying to tell a story with his music. And that's attractive to me. I don't know why."

There's a kind of freedom in that, I suggested. In not being able to pin something down or explain it.

"Mm-hmm," he said.

"That's the way I feel about your drawings," I said. "With a photograph of a supposedly real thing, people feel more equipped to say it means *this* or it means *this*."

"When, actually, it's often quite abstract," Eggleston said. "As you notice when you look at them upside down."

"Like the way you can see just a fragment of a side of a building in your picture and know it's in New Orleans. To even say exactly why that is, is hard to describe."

"Yes, that's absolutely true," Eggleston allowed.

I turned to Andra. "And growing up, he played for you?" I asked. She nodded, her father's coat still wrapped around her shoulders. "Oh, all the time. He didn't know he was playing for me, but he was. He still is."

*Editor's note: *William Eggleston: Democratic Camera, Photographs and Video, 1961–2008* was presented at the Whitney Museum of American Art in New York, November 7, 2008–January 25, 2009.

Originally published as two separate stories, in *New York* magazine on October 30, 2008, and on Vogue online on February 20, 2017.

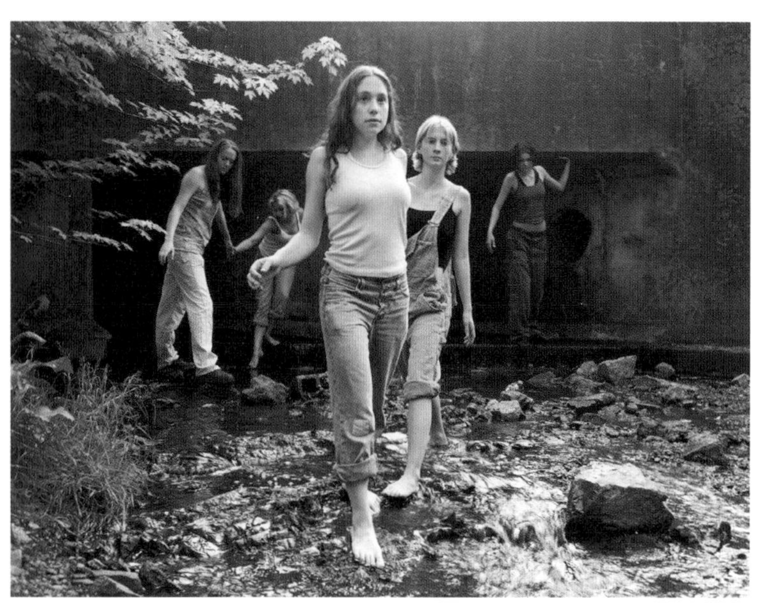

Justine Kurland, *The Wall*, 2000

The Jeremys: A Short Story for Justine Kurland's "Girl Pictures"

The girls were rebelling. The girls were acting out. The girls had run away from home, that much was clear. They were trying on a version of themselves that the world had thus far shown them was "boy." Floating a raft down the Mississippi. Tucking smokes into the sleeve of a T-shirt. Having a rumble. Living off the land. Cowboys, sailors, pirates, hitchhikers, hobos, train hoppers, explorers, catchers in the rye, lords of the flies—you name it, all the dominion of boys. If you wanted a place in the narrative, you had to imagine yourself inside of it.

You went to the edges. The girls were reclaiming a landscape that had been left for dead. Hiking to the hillcrest where the gleaming heads of satellite dishes hovered over the ridge like suburban aliens, like thrust-out flowers. Loitering in the marsh down where the tugboats parked for the night. Ripping off the doors of the rusted, wheel-less sedans, those capitalist relics. The doors seriously just came off in your hand. A flattened Plymouth became a fortress, someone's old crushed lipsticked loosies in the floorboards, tape spooling out of old cassettes, perfume archived in the upholstery. They wore anachronisms; hoodies and once-white tank tops and jeans with muddied hems and grass-stained legs; they could be from any era, any time; they could morph to be any tale.

They remained girls, when they were in the mood. Victorian

collectors of fairies and butterflies, wispy and impulsive, a passed-out *Picnic at Hanging Rock*, drunk on sun and hallucinating on the weird whorls that appeared when they stared too long into thin air. They were tough and wily; they were Mona stomping down the road in *Vagabond*, they were the lone chicks in *Over the Edge*. They were Pre-Raphaelite, postapocalyptic; they were punk, they were pastoral. But they didn't know any of this yet, not back then.

*

Always we went by fake names. Boy names, girl names, names people didn't have around here, prissy names for grown-ups who asked if our mothers knew where we were. (*"Your* mother," muttered the youngest of us.) If it was a cop asking, a different fake name. If it was a creep, we made him buy us Blizzards and cones and then we jumped the fence and ran away. Privately we all shared a name, Jeremy, after a boy we secretly crushed on, a boy who won the county spelling bee but had detention when they gave out the trophy. A boy who'd pierced a crucifix through his ear till it bled on his school desk, who'd brought weed to grade school, whose mother's name was on all the bad-checks lists at the grocery registers around town. We were all Jeremy. We couldn't decide if we loved him or if we wanted to be more like him, or both.

Because it wasn't that we wanted to *be* boys, necessarily. We wanted to plagiarize their stories. We pulled up their stakes, and plunged ours in.

This is us, Appalachian foothills. Pretend it's anywhere. Three sets of sisters, out in the woods, deep in a ravine. We built forts; suspended ourselves from trees; shed our clothes and jumped in a swimming hole that gaped in the cold creek, clear to its sandy floor. It was so cold we screamed; we lay on the rocks afterward to dry like snakes in the sun. The sky was often murky in those summers. The blue haze of the mountains and the shapes of houses showed dimly and faraway through the trees, through the cascades of kudzu that covered it all in a beautiful green disease.

No one came here. No one we saw or heard. Sometimes there were traces: a washing machine tumbled down a gully, an abandoned grocery cart, slashed couch under a vine-strung ceiling to make a derelict living room, cans in the weeds, plastic bags stuck on branches, billowing like let go birthday balloons.

But this was our place, and it had a name, too, letters stitched together from our real names to make an unpronounceable sound like muffled wind. No matter where we were, if the air whistled right, we could hear it calling us. It was illegal among us to speak its name aloud, even if we could.

There were rituals, of course. We pricked our fingers with pocketknives and let the blood run bright and red down the rocks. We coughed on cigarettes trying for smoke rings, stuffed the soft pack in a plastic wrap, buried it under pine needles in the hollow of a tree for later or for someone else. When the third Jeremy lost the lighter, when we dropped the matches in the creek, it was still okay. After-school television had taught us that a pair of glasses could catch dry grass on fire if the sun struck right.

We were thrilled by darkness, longed for it, waited for it to descend, sought it everywhere.

*

Jeremys one and two couldn't be more different, secret and sure. Jeremys five and six had spent their first years on a farm, they were used to large animals and predators and snakes that showed up in the garden. "Honestly, you guys, they just sort of writhe around and go away," the sixth Jeremy said. "They're probably hatching in our midst right now." Three and four were the troublemakers. Young at sleepovers, they had made us run in the driveway and flash our nightgowns at passing cars. If they beeped, we flipped.

We went to the tunnel after two weeks of heavy rain, on the first day the sun returned through the fog. Two of the Jeremys had woken one morning to a dog barking at the rising water in their parents' kitchen. The rest of us lived on higher ground. We stole through sodden backyards, peeled through curtains of leaves, hopped the fallen branches that had tumbled into the creekbed. We followed the creek to the bridge, where a tunnel ran under the highway, feeding creek to river. In a solemn trespass, we marched single file toward the hoop of light at the other end, and toward the roar of the rapids. Shoes laced together, looped over our shoulders or left on the muddy bank behind us, the tunnel floor too slick to travel.

The darkness cloaked around us. We rolled our jeans to our knees. We sang because we were scared, though we'd never admit it aloud. Dumb songs and theme songs and jingles we'd unconsciously memorized and hymns forced on us, and songs we taped off the radio, missing the first few notes. We sang to hear the eerie echo of our voices bounce off the sides of the tunnel, mingle with the plonk of the water's slow drip, off the rumble of traffic far above. We stood at the far end of the tunnel and looked over the edge at the river below.

The second Jeremy was the strongest, and she went first like a climber, hand over hand along the slippery rocks that did for a shore, laughing at the muddy current that rushed below. With a long snapped branch she coaxed us forward, dragged us from tunnel to ground in a one-girl tug-of-war. We screamed as she pulled us into the light, gasped in the air of the other side, the rush of the water we just escaped, bare feet sinking into bright mud as we landed. From here the tunnel looked so high.

"We're never gonna be able to go back now," said the fourth Jeremy.

"Not that way anyway," said the second.

The river roared at our heels. Later we would tell ourselves we all tumbled out of the tunnel and never went back.

We traced the skinny path that ran along the riverbank, parallel to the trestle above, gravel scattering downhill when a freight train passed. The whistle blew mournfully at the highway crossing, at the bulkhead where we found enough dry sticks for a fire, set our muddy sneakers on stones, pictured a forever like this one: curling up on the rock formations of lonely state parks, hoarding packets of mustard and ketchup, scrubbing our T-shirts in rest-stop sinks with industrial pink soap; falling asleep to the ocean sounds of traffic and waking to a fury of horns.

*

When the sixth Jeremy got a boyfriend, we pinned him to the ground too. Kiss or spit, we commanded.

He wasn't as cute as the real Jeremy but he would do, for a while. He let us shoot his BB gun, led us out his attic window and onto his roof, as we stood barefoot on tar paper, holding each other up as we fired at the mountains of cans of beer his father drank night after night and flung into the yard.

*

Sometimes on those outside nights we speculated about the future, sometimes we measured the odds. Six Jeremys. We were a statistic. One in six was bound to become . . . something. One in six was bound to do . . . blank. One in six was bound to fall in love. No, we all wanted to fall in love. Get rich. Get married. ("Gross," said three Jeremys in near unison.) Get famous. Have babies. (Another chorus of "gross.") One in six of us will like girls. One in six of us will make something, discover something; one in six of us will do drugs, get sick, get hurt. One in six of us will be a criminal, one a teacher. One in six of us will never figure it out. One in six of us will never leave here. One in six of us is bound to disappear. One in six of us, she'll surprise you.

Sometimes the sky remained an unknowable white blank, revealing nothing. One day, the first Jeremy, out of nowhere, burst out: "How weird is it that I have a *uterus*!" We all cracked up.

Some days we were so bored we walked miles on the highway

for fun. A two-laner twisting up the mountain. Six whole miles to shoplift a Coke from the gas station. Cars passed us full of rhodo-dendron peepers, and men leered from spattered truck windows. When cars flew too fast around the curve we flung our bodies against the guardrail. We made faces in the distorted mirrors that marked the hairpin turns. We saw our reflections only like this: in glassy water, in dingy bathrooms, on hubcap chrome. We ran breakneck down the runaway truck ramp and let its humpbacked mountains of bulldozed dirt pillow us as we landed in time to watch the night turn purple and dark blue, pocked with stars.

Other times we ran to cement lots, roadside ditches, empty, forgotten fields. We stared at the south-lying mountains, the new black horizon where forest fires had blazed through the pines. We lay in the dirt dreaming, feeling the cold through our clothes, pinning ourselves between ground and bare sky. Thoughts rocked through our heads. Would you rather and what if. *What if they found us like this? Or like this?* We rearranged ourselves like a murder scene and laughed. In the winter we made violent snow angels in the drifts, whipping our arms to leave behind ragged, torn, weathered-looking wings.

Sometimes we thought we were the only ones. Sometimes we agreed there had to be others, like life on other planets. We imagined those Jeremys, far out there, the ones loitering in subway stations and roaming dangerous city neighborhoods. We couldn't fathom that they might ever want to be us, in our burnt forests and brown creeks and abandoned houses, on the edges of something too.

*

One in six, we'd always said, will move away. The color of the dirt there is different, red by the river's edge, alkaline gray in lawns worn free of grass. Fire ants and blue hibiscus wander the chain-link fence. When the third Jeremy tells the story of how she got there, no one believes her. How she'd driven six states away from the other Jeremys in a van with two guys and a freaked-out cat. How they got temporarily lost in a hill-country town called Utopia. How they'd slept on a rock formation made of pink granite that vibrated and sang in the cold. When she retells it, it sounds like a fairy tale she would have made up on the spot for the other Jeremys, during some night camped out in the broken-down Plymouth, way back when. Sometimes she thinks she walked through the tunnel and landed here years later instead.

Here is a back lot tucked in a part of town they haven't torn down yet, Jeremys roaming in and out, girl Jeremys and boy Jeremys alike. The boyfriend has disappeared, maybe, who can say. The other guy has become another Jeremy. Here they share houses on wheels, a church bus with the Jesus words painted over in black, three trailers covered in silver corrugated sheets, and a falling-down house no one goes into, except when it storms and the dogs run for the closets. The ground is gritty with broken nails and sawdust. It's a place of dirt and metal and the third Jeremy is as flat as metal, as thin as the guitar she plays, sitting in a rickety wheelchair rescued from a field. She still will never say aloud the name of the secret place of the Jeremys but sometimes she thinks she can hear it, carried in the wind. Sometimes when she thinks of growing up one of six, she sees that time, that place, as a fantasy. Sometimes she wonders if she made it up too. Mostly what she thinks about is this: how a girl at the center of a rebellious narrative was once considered a fantasy.

*

They reached a forlorn ravine where live oaks improbably still grew; a transplanted palm had accidentally managed to thrive. They squatted to piss in fields of Queen Anne's lace; they napped in apple orchards. One day they went to the beach where they made out with boys, with each other, whatever. They stayed there till the sun fell and the cold came on and then they figured out what to do next. Maybe they'd go home. Maybe they never would.

Didn't people survive in the woods, for like, months? They'd grow tanned, leathery, wild. They'd drink from streams. They'd forage. They'd learn to hunt. One girl claimed she could skin a squirrel, her uncle had taught her. This girl, she knew things. She'd show you.

Originally published in *Justine Kurland: Girl Pictures* (Aperture, 2020).

192

Index

Page references in *italics* refer to illustrations.

A

Abdul, Paula, 99

Acid Rain ("Mercy Mercy Me," Marvin Gaye) (Smith), *128*

Acuff, Roy, 114

Adams, Robert, 15–16, 153

The Adventures of Guille and Belinda and the Enigmatic Meaning of Their Dreams (Sanguinetti), 124

Agee, James, 11, 26–27, 28, 31–32, 146

AIDS, 69

Ailey, Alvin, 109–10

Alabama

    Hale County This Morning, This Evening (Ross), 136–37, 140, 145–47

    16th Street Baptist Church bombing (Birmingham, 1963), 165, 166

    South County, AL (a Hale County) (Ross), *132,* 135–36

Albright, Peggy, 62

Almereyda, Michael, 181

Als, Hilton, 161

Altman, Robert, 115

Alvarez-Smikle, Ramon, 166

ambiguity, 83–89

American Photographs (Evans), 26

The Americans (Frank), 30, 152, 155

American Sign Language, 23, 33

American West (Avedon), 162

analog photography, 74

Andersen, Hans Christian, 122

Anderson, André, 96

Anderson, Laurie, 70

Anderson, Sherwood, 31

Aperture, 152, 176

Aperture magazine, 57, 65

Apsáalooke (Crow), 59–60, 62

Arbery, Ahmaud, 148

Arbus, Diane, 15, 17, 41, 55, 108, 151, 172–73

Argentina, 10, 121, 122

Armstrong, David, 69, 74–75, 76

Arrival in America, 1996 (Markosian), *46*

Art Institute of Chicago, 168

El asador (Sanguinetti), *125*

Atget, Eugène, 16, 17, 26

Austerlitz (Sebald), 87, 88

Avedon, Richard, 15, 110, 162, 163

B

B-17 Flying Fortress, *58*, 67

"Baby, Baby, Baby" (Prince), 97

Bach, Johann Sebastian, 180, 182

Bad Boy, Julia (Her Dreams Are True), 62

Baldwin, James, 108, 110, 165

The Ballad of Sexual Dependency (Goldin), 69–70, 71–80

Bancroft Library (University of California, Berkeley), 152, 158

BART, 158

Barthes, Roland, 85

BdotCroc, 96

Bearden, Romare, 109, 110

The Beautiful Ones (Prince), 97

Belasco, Eyde, 50

Belorusets, Yevgenia, 82–89

In the Face of War, 86–87

Lucky Breaks, *82*, *83*, 84–86, 87

Modern Animal, 85

"My Sister," 84

"The Seer of Dreams," 88–89

"The Stars," 84

Zhyvy Kutochok (The Living Corner), 85

Berger, John, 27–28

Bergman, Ingmar, 76

Bergson, Henri, 144

Berlin, Lucia, 141–42, 155

Bertolucci, Bernardo, 76

Bey, Dawoud, 10, 161–68

Dawoud Bey: An American Project (Whitney Museum of American Art, 2021), 161–62, 166–67

Birmingham Project, 166

Class Pictures, 165

Evergreen, 167

Harlem Redux, 165

Night Coming Tenderly, Black, 166–67, 168

9.15.63, 166

Seeing Deeply, 163

Street Portraits, 162

In This Here Place, 167

Untitled #20 (Farmhouse and Picket Fence I), 129

A Young Man Resting on an Exercise Bike, Amityville, NY, 160

Biggie Smalls, 164

Biley, DeFord, 114

Birmingham Project (Bey), 166

Blackburn, Emmet, 57

Black people, 163, 167

violence against, 147–48, 165–66

We Wanted a Revolution: Black Radical Women, 1965–85 (Brooklyn Museum, 2017), 108

Bland, Michael, 91

Bland, Sandra, 148

Bowery Hotel (New York City), 176

Bowie, David, 98

Boys Flying, Amesville, Ohio (Rexroth), *54*

Bracey, Sunshine, 162, 164

Brassaï, 109

Broken Manual (Soth), 25–26

Brooklyn, 164–65

Brooklyn Museum, 108

Brooks, Rayshard, 148

Brothers Grimm, 122

Brown, James, 69, 104

Brown, Jericho, 133

Brutti, Emanuele, 135, 136, 139, 143

Bryant, Quincy, 145

Bullowa, Arthur, 153

Burnaugh-Johnson, Alda, 103

But Still, It Turns (International Center of Photography, 2021), 133–49

Byrne, David, 180

C

Cage, John, 30, 41–42

Cahiers du Cinéma, 76

Caldwell, Joseph, 40, 41, 44

Callas, Maria, 69

Campany, David, 28

Cane (Toomer), 146

Carter, Jimmy, 137, 176

Carter Family, 114

Cartier-Bresson, Henri, 179

Carver, Raymond, 28, 155

Casale, Bob, 99

Cash, Johnny, 114, 116, 117

Casotti, Piergiorgio, 135, 136, 139, 143

Castelli Graphics, 76

Cather, Willa, 31

CBS Records, 77

CBS Sunday Morning, 181

Center for Documentary Studies, 29, 39

Champagne, 96

Chauvin, Derek, 147–48, 166

Chelsea Hotel (New York), 173

Chevron, 156

Choi, Richard, 135, 136, 143–44

Christenberry, William, 146

Chuang, Joshua, 15

Cincinnati Art Museum, 57

cinema, 76

Clark, Larry, 70

Clark, Sebastian, 85

Clash, 77

Class Pictures (Bey), 165

Clayton, Paul, 116–17

Cline, Patsy, 114

Clinton, George, 94

CNN, 176

Cochran, Hank, 115

Coen brothers, 117

Cole, Teju, 137

Coles, Robert, 28–30

Collins, Addie Mae, 165

Collins, Daniel, 145

Collins, Sarah Jean, 165

COLORS magazine, 29

Columbia University, 156

Complexity (Rexroth), 55

Condé Nast Publications, 40

Controversy, 97

Cooke, Sam, 171

Cookie at Tin Pan Alley (Goldin), *68*

Cooper, Amy, 148

Cooper, Christian, 148

Cooper, Stoney, 118

Cooper Union, 40, 41

Cosindas, Marie, 153

Cotter, Holland, 108

Cotton Tenants (Agee), 27

country music, 115, 116–19

COVID-19 pandemic, 141–42

Crawford, Joan, 76

Crockett, Daisha, 95

Crockett, Robin, 95–96

Crow (Apsáalooke), 59–60, 62

Crow Indian Reservation, 59, 61–62

Curtis, Edward S., 60–61

Cymone, André, 96

C.Z. and Max on the Beach, Truro, Mass. (Goldin), *126*

D

Dad on Bed (Sultan), 52

Dakota Access Pipeline, 124

Davidson, Bruce, 17

Davis, Bette, 76

Davis, Llewyn (character), 117

Dawes Act, 60

Day, Morris, 96

D&D Bail Bonds (Wichita Falls, Texas), 171

Dean, James, 171

DeCarava, Roy, 110, 136–37, 138, 163, 167

Delano, Jack, 146

DeLillo, Don, 174

democratic photography, 172

   The Democratic Forest (David Zwirner Gallery, 2017), 177–79

   William Eggleston: Democratic Camera, Photographs and Video, 1961–2008 (Whitney Museum of American Art, 2008–2009), 171–72

"Developing My Pictures" (Jones), 115

Devo, 99

Diana camera, 55, 56, 57

Dick, Vivienne, 72

Dickens, Little Jimmy, 114, 116

Didion, Joan, 42–43, 147, 152

Dietz, Howard, 24

digital photography, 74–75, 143

Dirty Mind (Prince), 98

Diving for Pearls (Goldin), 74–75

documentary methods, 84, 138

Dog, Mr., 41

Dolly Parton, Symphony Hall, Boston, Massachusetts (Horenstein), *112*, 119

DoubleTake magazine, 28–30, 39

Draper, Lou, 110

DuBois, Doug, 50

Duke University, 29, 39, 41

Dunne, John Gregory, 147

Dybek, Stuart, 29

Dyer, Geoff, 39

Dylan, Bob, 117

E

Eagle Rock Reservation, 20–21

Eastman Kodak, 17

Eckists, 101–2

The Effects of Technology on the Individual: Photographs by Chauncey Hare (MoMA, 1977), 151–52

Eggleston, Andra, 176, 180, 181, 182–83

Eggleston, Rosa Dossett, 173, 179, 181, 182

Eggleston, William (Bill), 10, 28, 123, 151, 153, 171–83

   The Democratic Forest (David Zwirner Gallery, 2017), 177–79

   William Eggleston: Democratic Camera, Photographs and Video,

1961–2008 (Whitney Museum of American Art, 2008–2009), 171–72

William Eggleston: Portraits (National Gallery, 2015), 178

William Eggleston in the Real World (Almereyda), 181

William Eggleston's Guide (MoMA, 1976), 173

Election Eve, 137–38, 176

Graceland pictures, 173–75

Los Alamos (Foam, 2015), 178

Stranded in Canton, 173, 180

Untitled (ca. 1971), *170*

Untitled (ca. 1983–86), *131*

Eggleston, William III, 180

Eggleston, Winston, 174, 181

Eggleston Artistic Trust, 171, 180

Election Eve (Eggleston), 137–38, 176

Electric Fetus, 100

Elgort, Arthur, 110

The Emigrants (Sebald), 87

England, Helen, 154, 157

England, Orville, 152, 154, 157

Environmental Protection Agency (EPA), 157

Eurana Park (Ross), *12*, *14*, *17*, *18*

Evans, Walker, 20, 28, 31–32, 41, 65, 156–57

   American Photographs, 26

   Let Us Now Praise Famous Men (Agee and Evans), 11, 26–27, 146

   "Six Days at Sea" (Agee and Evans), 28

   Walker Evans: First and Last (1978), 152

Evergreen (Bey), 167

Evers, Medgar, 148

F

The Family (Schiele), 144

Farm Security Administration (FSA), 31, 65, 146

Faulkner, William, 28

Fellini, Federico, 76

fiction, 83–89

film, 76

Finding Nemo, 100

First Avenue (Minneapolis), 93

flash back, 144

Fletcher, Suzanne, 69

Floyd, George, 147–48, 166

Floyd, Pretty Boy, 117

Foam (Amsterdam), 178

Fonvielle, Lloyd, 137–38

For a Love of His People: The Photography of Horace Poolaw (National Museum of the American Indian, 2014), 63

Foreverence, 99

Forever Your Girl (Abdul), 99

Fortune magazine, 27, 28

found photography, 88

Frank, Robert, 30, 152, 155

Friedlander, Lee, 41, 151, 153, 172–73

Friedlander, Maria, 40–41

Fundación Mapfre (Madrid), 14, 21

"Funk Machine" (Prince), 104

future present, 147–48

G

Galassi, Peter, 79

Galileo, 141

Garbo, Greta, 76

Gaultier, Jean Paul, 180

Gaye, Marvin, *128*

Gay Men's Health Crisis, 41

Gedney, William Gale, 10, 28, 29, 30, 39–4

   A Time of Youth: San Francisco, 1966–1967, 38, 41–44

   What Was True: The Photographs of William Gedney (Sartor and Dyer, eds.), 39

Gefter, Philip, 42

Genitempo, Matthew, 140

Gibson, William, 31

Gini Index, 139

Giraud, Brian, 98

Girl Pictures (Kurland), 185–92

Goldberg, Jim, 51–52

Goldin, Nan, 10, 69–80, 122

   The Ballad of Sexual Dependency, 69–70, 71–80

   Cookie at Tin Pan Alley, 68

   C.Z. and Max on the Beach, Truro, Mass., *126*

   Diving for Pearls, 74–75

Gordon, Bette, 77

Gossage, John, 19

Gould, Glenn, 9

Gowdy, Barbara, 123

Graceland, 173–75

Graceland Holdings, 98–99

Graham, Paul, 16, 135, 141

Grand Central, 96

Grand Ole Opry, 113–14, 115, 117

Graves, Milford, 163

A Graveyard and Steel Mill in Bethlehem, Pennsylvania (Evans), 20

Great Depression, 31, 146

Guggenheim Foundation, 18, 152, 154, 156

Guthrie, Woody, 117

H

Hale County This Morning, This Evening (Ross), 136–37, 140, 145–47

Hall, Tom T., 115

Halpern, Gregory, 16, 135, 136, 140–41

Hampton, James, 34–36

Hamptonese, 35–36

Hansberry, Lorraine, 165

Hare, Chauncey, 10, 151–58

   The Effects of Technology on the Individual: Photographs by Chauncey Hare (MoMA, 1977), 151–52

   Interior America (1978), 152, 155, 156–57

   Protest Photographs (2009), 153, 156

   Suburbia (1973), 156

   This Was Corporate America (1984), 156

   West Chester, Pennsylvania, *150*, 155

   Work Abuse: How to Recognize and Survive It (Hare and Wyatt), 157

Harlem, 163

Harlem Redux (Bey), 165

Harlow, Jean, 76

Harper's Bazaar, 28

Harrington, Richard, 175

Harris, Alex, 28–30

Hasselblad camera, 123

Hatleberg, Curran, 136

   Lost Coast, 135, 140–41, 143

   Lost Coast (26), *127*

Hawkins, Screamin' Jay, 69

Heaney, Seamus, 28–29

Hébel, François, 71

Heiferman, Marvin, 76

Hendrix, Jimi, 97

Her Dreams Are True (Julia Bad Boy), 62

Here, 2012 (Ross), *132*

Hicks, Leanna, 179, 181

High Museum (Atlanta), 161–62

Hine, Lewis, 17

Histories: Tales from the '70s (Horenstein), 115–16

Hollywood, 52, 91, 99

Honky Tonk: Portraits of Country Music (Horenstein), 115, 116–19

Horenstein, Henry, 70, 115

   Dolly Parton, Symphony Hall, Boston, Massachusetts, 112

   Histories: Tales from the '70s, 115–16

   Honky Tonk: Portraits of Country Music, 115, 116–19

Horton, Johnny, 116

House of Coates (Soth and Zellar), 30–31

House of Day, House of Night (Tokarczuk), 88

Howard, Harlan, 115

Hughes, Langston, 138, 167

Hujar, Peter, 85

Hume, Richard P., 153

I

IIT Institute of Design, 17

Imnadze, Ana, 50–51

Index G (Casotti and Brutti), 135, 139, 143

Indian Health Service, 59

Indian New Deal, 64

Instagram, 30

Interior America (Hare), 152, 155, 156–57

Interior of the Best Indian Kitchen on the Crow Reservation (Throssel), 61–62

International Center of Photography, 122, 133–49

In the Face of War (Belorusets), 86–87

In This Here Place (Bey), 167

Inventing My Father (Markosian), 53

Iossel, Mikhail, 48

IOWA (Rexroth), 55–57

Iris Garden (Soth), 30

Isolarii, 85, 87

Ives, Charles, 43

J

Jarmusch, Jim, 75

Jehovah's Witness, 92

"The Jeremys," 185–92

La Jetée (Marker), 75

Jeu de Paume, 86

Joel, Billy, 98

Johnson, Denis, 34–35, 36

Jones, Gene, 51

Jones, George, 114, 115

Jones, Grace, 109

Jones, Tom, 63

Junior M.A.F.I.A., 164

K

Kadan, Nikita, 87

Kalman, Tibor, 29

Kamoinge, 110

Steven Kasher Gallery, 108

Kelly, Ed, 35

June Kelly Gallery, 108

Khomenko, Lesia, 87

Killip, Chris, 16

Kilmister, Lemmy, 99

King, Martin Luther, Jr., 146, 148

Kiowa community, 62–65, 66–67

Kiowa George, 63

Kismaric, Susan, 14, 15, 107

Klemp, Harold, 101–2

Klimt, Gustav, 144

Kristofferson, Kris, 115, 117

Kurland, Justine
    Girl Pictures, 185–92
    Toys R Us, 130
    The Wall, 184

L

Lamplighter Lounge (the Lamp, Memphis), 171

Lange, Dorothea, 65

The Last Days of W. (Soth), 25–26

The Last Son (Goldberg), 51–52

The Last Supper (da Vinci), 154

LBM Dispatch, 31, 32

Lê, An-My, 15

Lee, Spike, 92

Lee, Wilma, 118

Leica camera, 154, 176

Leonardo da Vinci, 154

Let Us Now Praise Famous Men (Agee and Evans), 11, 26–27, 146

Levitt, Helen, 151, 153

Lewis, Jerry Lee, 116

Life magazine, 65

Light, Ken, 156–57

Like a Prayer (Madonna), 99

Lin, Maya, 18

Lincoln, Albert and Mary, 59

Little Brown Mushroom, 26, 31, 32

Lolita (Nabokov), 32, 164

Los Alamos (Eggleston), 178

Lost Coast (Hatleberg), 135, 140–41, 143

Lost Coast (26) (Hatleberg), *127*

Louboutin, Christian, 180

Louvin Brothers, 114

Lovesexy (Prince), 98–99

Lowe, Harry, 35

Lucas, George, 99

Lucky Breaks (Belorusets), *82, 83,* 84–86, 87

M

MacDill Field (Tampa, Florida), 64

Madonna, 94, 99

Magnoli, Albert, 91

Maguire, Mitch, 99

Malcolm, Janet, 152

Manifest (Potter), 135

Mann, Sally, 74

Marcus, Greil, 174–75

Marker, Chris, 75

Markosian, David, 49

Markosian, Diana, 47–53
    Arrival in America, 1996, 46
    Inventing My Father, 53
    Mornings (With You), 53
    Santa Barbara, 46, 49–53

Markosian, Svetlana, 49, 52–53

Massaum (Animal Dance), 61

Matthews, Scott L., 146

Max Fish, 77

Maxwell, William, 28

McBride, Bunny, 66

McCarty, Lisa, 42

McCleary, Timothy, 61, 62

McNair, Denise, 165

Memphis, Tennessee, 171–75

Menschen des 20 Jahrhunderts (People of the 20th Century) (Sander), 15

Michals, Duane, 151

Milagros (Sanguinetti), *120*

Miller, Roger, 115

A Ming Breakfast: Grits and Scrambled Moments (Smith), 108

Minneapolis, Minnesota, *90*, 91–104

Mirrors and Windows: American Photography since 1960 (San Francisco Museum of Modern Art, 1979), 10, 151, 153

Mitchell, Joseph, 28

Model, Lisette, 15, 108, 110

Modern Animal (Belorusets), 85

Modernism, 144

Monk, Thelonious, 93

Monroe, Bill, 114

Moore, James, 110

Moore College of Art and Design, 17

Moravian College, 17

Morgan, J. P., 60

Mornings (With You) (Markosian), 53

Morris, Philip, 151, 153

Morrison, Toni, 168

Morrissey, Paul, 76

Motörhead, 99

The Movement (Hansberry), 165

Mozart, Wolfgang Amadeus, 180

Mrs. Dalloway (Woolf), 144

MTV News, 93

Mudd Club, 79

Mueller, Cookie, 68, 69, 74

Munch, Edvard, 144

Murray, David, 109

Museum of Modern Art (MoMA), 41, 79, 107–8

    The Effects of Technology on the Individual: Photographs by Chauncey Hare (1977), 151–52

    William Eggleston's Guide (1976), 173

    New Photography (1985), 13

    Pictures by Women: A History of Modern Photography (2010), 108

Myles, Lynda, 50

"My Sister" (Belorusets), 84

N

Nabokov, Vladimir, 32, 164

Nance, Marilyn, 164

Nashville, Tennessee, 113–19

Nashville Sound, 115

National Front, 73

National Gallery (London), 178

National Museum of the American Indian, 62, 63

Native American people, *58*, 59–62, 63–64, 66

Near Williston, North Dakota (Soth), *22*

Nelson, Kadir, 148

Nelson, Prince Rogers (Prince), 91–104

Nelson, Tyka, 95

Nelson, Willie, 114–15

New Orleans, Louisiana, 173, 178–79, 180

New Photography (MoMA, 1985), 13

New Power Generation, 91

New York City, New York, 176–83

New Yorker, 88, 148

New York Times, 108

New York Times Magazine, 137

Niagara (Soth), 25–26, 32–33

Nicolar, Lucy (Princess Watahwaso), 66

Niesp, Sharon, 69

Night Coming Tenderly, Black (Bey), 166–67, 168

9.15.63 (Bey), 166

1999 (Prince), 97

The North American Indian (Curtis), 60–61

Northern Cheyenne tribe, 61

O

Obama, Barack, 139

O'Connor, Flannery, 28

Office of Indian Affairs, 61

O'Grady, Megan, 144

Ohio, 31

Ohio State University, 56

Oji, 93

"Old Photographs" (Pride), 115

One Wall a Web (Wolukau-Wanambwa), 135, 148

Ono, Yoko, 69

On the Sixth Day (Sanguinetti), 121–24

Orlando: A Biography (Woolf), 133, 144

Ostashevsky, Eugene, 84

O'Toole, Erin, 51, 52

Our Present Invention (Wolukau-Wanambwa), 138–39

Owens, Bill, 156

P

Paisley Park, 94–95, 98–100

Palm magazine, 86

Palmer, Gus, *58*

pandemic time, 141–42

Paris, France, 179–80

Parks, Gordon, 108, 110

Parton, Dolly, *112*, 118–19

Penn, Irving, 15

Pepperdine University, 157

Percy, Walker, 28

Percy, Will, 30

Perlman, Carl, 77

Pharoah Sanders at the Bottom Line (Smith), *106*

pictorialism, 60

"A Picture of Me Without You" (Jones), 115

Pictures by Women: A History of Modern Photography (MoMA, 2010), 108

Pictures from Home (Sultan), 51, 52

"Pictures of Life's Other Side" (Williams), 115

Pifer, Florence, 60

Pittsburgh Steel, 154

Plenty Coups, 59–60

Point Richmond, California, 153

Polaroid photography, 32, 161

Poolaw, Bruce, 65, 66

Poolaw, Bryce, 63

Poolaw, Horace, 10, *58*, 62–67

Poolaw, Jerry, 63

Poolaw, John, 65

Poolaw, Linda, 63, 64–65

Poolaw, Robert, 63

Horace Poolaw Photography Project, 63

portrait photography, 15–16, 178

Potter, Kristine, 135, 136, 140, 143

Pratt Institute, 40

Charles Pratt Memorial Award, 19

present tense, 133–34

Presley, Elvis, 98, 116, 174, 175

Presley, Priscilla, 173–74

Pride, Charley, 114, 115

Prince, 91–104

protest, 10, 151–58

Protest Photographs (Hare), 153, 156

Protest the War (Ross), 19–20

Prymachenko, Maria, 86–87

Purple House, 97

Purple Rain (Prince), 91, 93, 97, 100

R

Ra, Sun, 109

racial violence, 147–48, 165–66

Rauschenberg, Robert, 35, 151

realism, 10, 151, 163

Red Star, Wendy, 62

Reed, Alda Le Shay, *90*, 102–3

Reeves, Del, 118

Reflecto, Dr. Randall, 173

Revolution of Dignity, 84

Rexroth, Nancy, 55–57

Richmond, Virginia, 138–39

Rimkus, Ulli, 77

The Rings of Saturn (Sebald), 87

Riverside Indian School, 64

Robbins, Marty, 114

Robertson, Carole, 165

Robinson, Johnny, 165

Rogers, Kenny, 98

Rolling Stone, 137

Romanticism, 60

Roma settlement, 84

Roosevelt, Franklin D., 64

Ross, Edward, 16, 19–20

Ross, Judith Joy, 10, 13–21

    Eurana Park (1982), *12*, 14, 17, 18

    Judith Joy Ross (Fundación Mapfre, 2022), 21

    Untitled (1982), *12*

Ross, RaMell

    Hale County This Morning, This Evening, 136–37, 140, 145–47

    Here, 2012, *132*

    South County, AL (a Hale County), *132*, 135–36

Rounder Records, 119

Rumors of War (Wiley), 138

Ryman Auditorium, 115, 117

S

Saint Louis, Missouri, 135, 139

Sander, August, 14–15, 17, 63

Sanders, Pharoah, *106*

San Francisco, California, *38*, 41–44

San Francisco Art Institute, 157

San Francisco Bay Guardian, 157

San Francisco Museum of Modern Art, 10, 51, 151, 153, 161–62

Sanguinetti, Alessandra, 10

The Adventures of Guille and Belinda and the Enigmatic Meaning of Their Dreams, 124

El asador, *125*

Milagros, *120*

On the Sixth Day, 121–24

Santa Barbara (Markosian), *46*, 49–53

Santa Barbara (NBC), 47–48, 49, 50, 53

Santana, Al, 164

Sartor, Margaret, 39

Schiele, Egon, 144

Schjeldahl, Peter, 149

Schwartz, Arthur, 24

Sebald, W. G., 30, 87, 88

Seeing Deeply (Bey), 163

"The Seer of Dreams" (Belorusets), 88–89

selfies, 97

"Sepulture South: Gaslight" (Faulkner), 28

Sessions, Roger, 43

Shampayne, 96

she dances on Jackson (Winship), 135

Shoemaker, Ferdinand, 61

Shore, Stephen, 151, 153

Shredded Wheat, 155

sign following, 138, 140–41

sign language, 33

Singer, Isaac Bashevis, 123

Siskind, Aaron, 17

"Six Days at Sea" (Agee and Evans), 28

The Slave (Singer), 123

Sleeping by the Mississippi (Soth), 25–26

Smikle, David Edward. *see* Bey, Dawoud

Smith, Eugene, 158

Smith, Jack, 76

Smith, Kiki, 76–77

Smith, Maggie, 76–77, 78

Smith, Ming, 107–11

Acid Rain ("Mercy Mercy Me," Marvin Gaye), *128*

A Ming Breakfast: Grits and Scrambled Moments, 108

Pharoah Sanders at the Bottom Line, *106*

Smith, Mingus, 109, 110

Smithsonian American Art Museum, 35

Smithsonian Folkways, 117

Solomon, Rosalind Fox, 152

Songbook (Soth), 24–26, 33

Soth, Alec, 30–33, *90*, 91, 92, 95, 100

Broken Manual, 25–26

House of Coates (Soth and Zellar), 30–31

Iris Garden, 30

The Last Days of W., 25–26

Near Williston, North Dakota, *22*

Niagara, 25–26, 32–33

Sleeping by the Mississippi, 25–26

Songbook, 24–26, 33

Soul of a Nation: Art in the Age of Black Power (Brooklyn Museum, 2018), 108

South County, AL (a Hale County) (Ross), *132*, 135–36

Spanish flu epidemic, 144

Springsteen, Bruce, 30

Standard Oil Company, 154, 156

Standing Rock Sioux, 124

Stanford University, 63, 64–65

"The Stars" (Belorusets), 84

Steidl and Pace/MacGill, 19–20

Sternfeld, Joel, 122

Stockhausen, Karlheinz, 43

Stranded in Canton (Eggleston), 173, 180

street photography, 163

Street Portraits (Bey), 162–65

Stryker, Roy, 31, 32

Stubbs, Ernie, 115

Studio 54, 109

Studio Museum (Harlem), 163

Suburbia (Hare), 156

Sultan, Irving, 52

Sultan, Larry, 51, 52

Szarkowski, John, 10, 14, 41, 107, 151, 154

T

Takayama, Miho, 93, 94, 100

Tate Modern, 108

Taylor, Breonna, 148

Telling a Crow Story: The Photographs of Richard Throssel (National Museum of the American Indian, 2003), 62

Temple of Eck, 101

Terkel, Studs, 28

Terminal 5, 70

This Was Corporate America (Hare), 156

Thoeny, Bret, 98

Thompson, E. P., 118

Thompson, Sonny, 91

The Throne (Hampton), 35

"The Throne of the Third Heaven of the Nations' Millennium General Assembly" (Johnson), 34–35, 36

Throssel, Richard, 10, 59–62, 65

Thunder Iron, 59

Thurmond, Strom, 18

time
But Still, It Turns (International Center of Photography, 2021), 133–49

pandemic time, 141–42

past-present, 137–38, 167

Time-Life Books, 40

A Time of Youth: San Francisco, 1966–1967 (Gedney), *38*, 41–44

Times Square Show (Colab, 1980), 72

Tin Pan Alley, 68, 76–78

Tokarczuk, Olga, 88

Toomer, Jean, 146

Tootsies Orchid Lounge (Nashville), 115, 117, 119

Top Cats III, 113

Toscani, Oliviero, 29

To the Lighthouse (Woolf), 144, 145

Toys R Us (Kurland), *130*

Tubb, Ernest, 114

Twitty, Conway, 116

Twombly, Cy, 74

U

Ukraine, 83, 84, 86

Underground Railroad, 167

Under the Cherry Moon (Prince), 99

United States Army Air Corps, 64

University of California, Berkeley, 152, 158

University of Minnesota, 94

Untitled (Eggleston, ca. 1971), *170*

Untitled (Eggleston, ca. 1983–86), *131*

Untitled (Ross), *12*

Untitled #20 (Farmhouse and Picket Fence I) (Bey), *129*

V

Van Der Zee, James, 110

van Sant, Gus, 180

Velvet Underground, 69

Vertigo (Sebald), 87

Vietnam War, 18

Virginia, 168

Viva, 173

Vogue magazine, 28

von Euw, Jack, 152, 153, 158

W

Wagoner, Porter, 119

Wainwright, Martha, 70

The Wall (Kurland), *184*

Wallace, Christopher "Notorious B.I.G.," 164

Ware, Virgil, 165

Warhol, Andy, 76, 151

Warner Bros. Records, 99–100

Princess Watahwaso (Lucy Nicolar), 66

Waters, John, 76

Wayne, John, 139

Weegee, 171

Wells, Kitty, 114

Welty, Eudora, 28, 178

Wesley, Cynthia, 165

Wessel, Henry, 153

West Chester, Pennsylvania (Hare), *150*, 155

We Wanted a Revolution: Black Radical Women, 1965–85 (Brooklyn Museum, 2017), 108

What Remains (Choi), 135, 143–44

What Was True: The Photographs of William Gedney (Sartor and Dyer, eds.), 39

White, Minor, 57

The White Bone (Gowdy), 123

White Noise (DeLillo), 174

Whitney Museum of American Art, 70, 76, 77

    Dawoud Bey: An American Project (2021), 161–62, 166–67

    William Eggleston: Democratic Camera, Photographs and Video, 1961–2008 (2008–2009), 171–72

wide-angle photography, 155

Wiley, Kehinde, 138

Williams, Bert, 140

Williams, Hank, 114, 115, 116

Williams, Joy, 9–11

Williams, William Carlos, 28

Willis, Deborah, 163

Wilson, August, 109

windows, 10

Winehouse, Amy, 79

Winesburg, Ohio (Anderson), 31

Wingo, Rebecca S., 61

Winogrand, Garry, 151, 172–73

Winship, Vanessa, 135, 136, 139–40

The Winter Garden Dispatch, 31

Wolukau-Wanambwa, Stanley, 136, 140, 143

    One Wall a Web, 135, 148

    Our Present Invention, 138–39

women photographers

    Pictures by Women: A History of Modern Photography (2010), 108

We Wanted a Revolution: Black Radical Women, 1965–85 (Brooklyn Museum, 2017), 108

Wood, James, 88

Woolf, Virginia, 133, 144, 145

Work Abuse: How to Recognize and Survive It (Hare and Wyatt), 157

Works Progress Administration (WPA), 28, 31

Wright, Daunte, 166

WSM 650 AM, 113

WWVA radio, 118

Wyatt, Judy, 157

X

X, Malcolm, 148

Y

Yablonska, Tetyana, 87

Yale University, 162

The Year of Magical Thinking (Didion), 147

A Young Man Resting on an Exercise Bike, Amityville, NY (Bey), *160*

Z

Zellar, Brad, 30–31, 32

Zhyvy Kutochok (The Living Corner) (Belorusets), 85

David Zwirner Gallery, 177–79, 180

ZZYZX (Halpern), 135, 136, 140–41

Acknowledgments

Strange Hours is a particularly apt title for a book whose pieces come from so many divergent places and times. Thanks to my editor Brendan Embser for the suggestion of the title and the proposal of the collection itself—and for his extraordinary guidance, vision, and openness. I am indebted to Susan Ciccotti for her terrifically good edits, to designer Adam Turnbull and the team at Pacific, to Matthew Leifheit for an inspired portrait session, to Varun Nayar for editorial support. Tremendous thanks to Joy Williams for her text here, for her wisdom and her writing as a whole, for workshops years ago and all since.

Aperture is the original home of many of these pieces, whether in magazine or book form, and home (present and past) to so many talented, wonderful editors and designers. In particular I wish to thank Michael Famighetti, Denise Wolff, Lesley A. Martin, Sarah Meister, Chris Boot, Nicole Acheampong, Paula Kupfer, Emily CM Anderson, and Karina Eckmeier.

I am grateful to the photographers in these and other pieces for our conversations, for the inclusion of their pictures, and collaborations and friendship. Thank you Alessandra Sanguinetti, Dawoud Bey, Ming Smith, Justine Kurland, Alec Soth, Nan Goldin, Henry Horenstein, Kristine Potter, Nancy Rexroth, Diana Markosian, Judith Joy Ross, Paul Graham, RaMell Ross, Curran Hatleberg, Gregory Halpern, Vanessa Winship, Richard Choi,

Stanley Wolukau-Wanambwa, Emanuele Brutti, and Piergiorgio Casotti, Yevgenia Belorusets, and William Eggleston. Many thanks to the Eggleston Artistic Trust and David Zwirner for the photograph on the cover of this book.

Thanks also to the editors of pieces in their first incarnation and others who made their publication possible: Laura Regensdorf, Suzanne Shaheen, Abby Aguirre, Alessandra Codinha, Jessie Heyman, Alexandra Macon, Chioma Nnadi, Sally Singer, Alex Zafiris, Sara Roffino, David Haskell, Folake Ologunja, Michael Mack, Liz Constable-Maxwell, Joshua Chuang, Wendy Red Star, Linda Poolaw, Ethan Jones, Caitlin Kelly, Lisa McCarty, Monika Condrea, and New Directions Publishing. Thanks to everyone who invited Alec Soth and me into their homes, the places where Prince once lived.

A book like this can't possibly hold all of the writings on photography, nor all the photographers, living and gone, whose work has been so important to me. Grateful for conversations (and in some cases collaborations) with: Susan Meiselas, Joel Sternfeld, Carolyn Drake, Andres Gonzalez, Jim Goldberg, Mitch Epstein, Rineke Dijkstra, Danny and Nancy Lyon, Juliana Paciulli, Carrie Schneider, Katsu Naito, Victor Blue, Jason Fulford, David Campany. Thank you, Thomas Gebremedhin, Diego Hadis, Eviana Hartman, Andrew Chan, Anna Thorngate, Durga Chew-Bose, Danielle Jackson, Jackie Bates, and Matthew Schnipper.

To all my communities originating from North Carolina, Austin, and New York. And for input on aspects of this book in particular (whether they were aware of it or not at the time), thanks to Rachel Blackwell, Diana Welch, Jim McHugh, Michael Parker, Cyrus Moussavi, Brittany Nugent, Dave Tompkins, Alexa Dilworth, Becca Cohen, Rosie Rosenthal, Morgan Coy, Michelle Marchesseault, Julie Burgardt, Julia Rommel, Donilee McGinnis, Zach Blue, Lorna Vetters, John McManus, Betsey Fortlouis, Karen Ingram, Louise Bauso, Eric Amling, Sarah Grimm, Matt LaFleur, Dave Tompkins, Sarah Shackelford Buck, Josh Rubin, Ashleigh Bryant Phillips, Jessie Gaynor, Thessaly La Force, Marya Spence,

Paul Rusconi, Nate Heiges, Karen Davidson, and Alix Ohlin.

I am grateful for the support of MacDowell, Atlantic Center for the Arts, Magnum Foundation, Archive of Documentary Arts, Michener Center for Writers, Djerassi, and to S. B. Cooper and Rebecca Besson, FotoFocus, Michael Hoeh, and Charlotte Carroll Tracy.

This is for my family, especially my parents Mary Jo and Archie, my sister Joanna Welborn, and Matt and Ike, Carol and Bryan; for W.S.E., Q.S.J., and C.N.J. and those in the stars. Thank you more than I can say. — Rebecca Bengal

Strange Hours: Photography, Memory, and the Lives of Artists
Selected Writings by Rebecca Bengal

Front cover: William Eggleston, *Untitled*, ca. 1970–73

Editor: Brendan Embser
Designer: Adam Turnbull, Pacific
Production Director: Minjee Cho
Production Managers: Andrea Chlad, Karina Eckmeier
Production Consultant: Thomas Bollier
Assistant Editor: Varun Nayar
Senior Text Editor: Susan Ciccotti
Proofreader: Isla Ng

Additional staff of the Aperture book program includes:
Sarah Meister, Executive Director; Lesley A. Martin, Creative Director; Taia Kwinter, Publishing Manager; Emily Patten, Publishing Associate; Michael Famighetti, Editor, *Aperture* magazine; Kellie McLaughlin, Chief Sales and Marketing Officer; Richard Gregg, Sales Director, Books

Special thanks:
This project was made possible, in part, with generous support from the Besson/Cooper Fund, FotoFocus, Michael Hoeh, and Charlotte Carroll Tracy.

This volume is part of *Aperture Ideas: Writers and Artists on Photography*, a series devoted to the finest critical and creative minds exploring key concepts in photography.

aperture
548 West 28th Street, 4th Floor
New York, NY 10001
aperture.org

Aperture, a not-for-profit foundation, connects the photo community and its audiences with the most inspiring work, the sharpest ideas, and with each other—in print, in person, and online.

First edition, 2023
Printed in China by Toppan
10 9 8 7 6 5 4 3 2 1

Library of Congress Control Number: 2022058015
ISBN 978-1-59711-554-4

To order Aperture books, or inquire about gift or group orders, contact:
orders@aperture.org

For information about Aperture trade distribution worldwide, visit:
aperture.org/distribution

APERTURE IDEAS

Writers and Artists on Photography

The Pleasures of Good Photographs
Essays by Gerry Badger

Light Matters: Writings on Photography
Essays by Vicki Goldberg

Crisis of the Real: Writings on Photography
Essays by Andy Grundberg

*Between the Eyes: Essays on
Photography and Politics*
By David Levi Strauss
Introduction by John Berger

John Berger: Understanding a Photograph
Edited and introduced by Geoff Dyer

In Our Own Image
Essays by Fred Ritchin

*Bending the Frame: Photojournalism,
Documentary, and the Citizen*
By Fred Ritchin

*Words Not Spent Today Buy Smaller Images Tomorrow:
Essays on the Present and Future of Photography*
By David Levi Strauss

Photography After Frank
Essays by Philip Gefter

*We Were Here: Sexuality,
Photography, and Cultural Difference*
Selected Writings by Sunil Gupta